Administrative Law for the 21st Century

Suzana Tavares da Silva

Administrative Law for the 21st Century

Administrative Law on an Illiberal and Post-Democratic Context

Springer

Suzana Tavares da Silva
Faculty of Law
University of Coimbra
Coimbra, Portugal

ISBN 978-3-031-55794-1 ISBN 978-3-031-55795-8 (eBook)
https://doi.org/10.1007/978-3-031-55795-8

This Springer imprint is published by the registered company Springer Nature Switzerland AG
The registered company address is: Gewerbestrasse 11, 6330 Cham, Switzerland

Preface

This monograph is not intended to be a manual of administrative law nor a systematic study of this branch of law nor even a synthesis of the state of the art of the new doctrinal proposals for this branch of law. It has much more modest aims. It simply aims to be a discursive reflection on the current challenges facing administrative law based on a key idea: the defence of the liberal model of society.

This is a reflection that brings together the contributions of our professional activity, firstly as teachers of public law (constitutional, administrative and tax) for around 20 years, as a judge at the Portuguese Supreme Administrative Court for almost 5 years and as a student of comparative public law and the challenges that globalisation and Europeanisation have raised for this area of law.

The "discomfort" or "misunderstanding" of the evolution of public law became more evident with the emergence of the 2008 financial crisis. In the EU member states most affected—including Portugal—the financial crisis gave rise to a legal crisis, caused by the "imposed" measures and the "hardening" of the policy of balancing the budget and reducing public debts. Even for countries that were not bailed out, this policy brought tighter rules, such as the need to submit the annual solutions adopted by member states in budgetary matters to the European institutions for scrutiny.

What were once "case studies"—such as the "threats" of "German resistance" to solutions that reduced national sovereignty imposed by the European Treaties, which deepened the solution of legal integration—became structured political movements contesting Europeanisation and economic globalisation. These political movements were mostly formed in the areas of left-wing ideology, i.e. against the model of privatisation and liberalisation of the economy. From their growth to the implosion of the classic political party systems in the countries of the European Union, a very short period of time elapsed.

This was followed, still in the context of Europeanisation, by the adoption of a set of increasingly demanding and interfering European policies that were less and less consensual in society, with particular emphasis on asylum and immigration policy. The context of the negative economic cycle, combined with the terrorist attacks, has led to political dissent driving social dissent and contributing to galvanising political contestation with the emergence of new parties. This time the political party changes came in the area of right-wing ideology, associated with the ideas of nationalism, security and national sovereignty.[1]

The media in Western countries, increasingly focused on ancillary facts and the instrumentalisation of affections and emotions, has distracted citizens from their essential problems and neutralised potential revolts. But we have entered, almost unnoticed, into a Manichean and not very tolerant society, into social tribalism, into the digitalisation of life, into the inability to regulate dematerialised economic and financial areas. Today we are faced with a world that we are no longer able to grasp, understand, rationalise and govern transparently.

And things got worse with the pandemic and the measures adopted to manage public health. While lockdowns have bought scientific research the time it needed to save lives with vaccines, isolation and the forced digitalisation of life have accelerated social disruption and conflict. At the same time, the slowdown in the economy has exacerbated inequalities in the global distribution of income and impoverished the West.

The aftermath of the pandemic has been even more catastrophic, as demonstrated by the wars in which we have found ourselves involved, the clamour over the climate crisis and the risks of artificial intelligence. For almost a decade, events have seemed to run roughshod over state political power. The democratic state, as we conceived it in the last half of the twentieth century and perfected it to ensure values essential to life in the community, such as equality and justice, today seems to be an impotent and meaningless institution. This is one of the driving forces behind populism. This is the main reason for the crisis in administrative law.

Our work, as we have said, attempts at identifying functional disruptions in administrative law, from the perspective of a European Union member state like Portugal, but looking at these disruptions in general terms. We start from an interesting debate that has been held in recent years by European and North American authors about the regulatory deficiencies of the current *status quo*, like the discrediting of democratic constitutionalism; we discuss the classic concepts of European *civil law administrative law*; and we end with the formulation of some proposals.

Coimbra, Portugal — Suzana Tavares da Silva

[1] *Sovereignty* is a concept that has evolved significantly since Jean Bodin and the unlimited power of the sovereign, passing through the dichotomy of national sovereignty and popular sovereignty, to culminate in the "shared" sovereignty of the moderns, which, in its own way, deconstructed the idea of power in autonomy—Morgado M (2021) Sovereignty. Dom Quixote, Lisbon.

Contents

Chapter 1
The "Idea" of Administrative Law

The "idea of" administrative law is a product of nineteenth-century liberal constitutionalism. We are referring to continental legal systems where administrative law can be defined as a set of rules and principles that ensure, within the framework of the rule of law, that administrative activity (exercised by administrative bodies or by private individuals to whom that exercise has been "delegated") is subject to the law and respects the fundamental rights of citizens. However, the idea of administrative law is not only the result of various historical and multidisciplinary *approaches*, but its autonomisation as a branch of law is also more recent. What is more, the constitutionalism of the second half of the twentieth century and the "generalisation" of fundamental rights ended up giving it an ultimate meaning and, in its own way, also a reason to jeopardise its essence.

Doctrine is not unanimous on the relationship it establishes between constitutional law and administrative law. Some authors suggest an understanding of administrative law as a "by-product" of concretised constitutional law. Others argue that it is an autonomous or emancipated right.[1] Without prejudice to the importance of this relationship, it seems to us that it ends up leading to an overly standardised view of the concept of administrative law and that, for this reason, it should be complemented: firstly, with reference to the evolution of the "idea of" administrative law (and public administration) in comparative terms and, then, with the identity of administrative *law in the* context of the differences and similarities between the continental (French) and *common law* models.

In the recent evolution of administrative law, several moments stand out. Firstly, the expansion of the welfare state and the (corresponding) administrative law of the provider state (using public and private law as a subsidiser, purchaser and contractualiser). Later, the widespread privatisation of economic sectors (especially traditional public services), which brought with it the administrative law of

[1] Wollenschläger (2017), pp. 7–10; Ginsburg (2017), pp. 60–71.

S. Tavares da Silva, *Administrative Law for the 21st Century*,
https://doi.org/10.1007/978-3-031-55795-8_1

economic regulation, with new players (administrative regulatory bodies as "independent authorities") and new legal principles (of competition, transparency, the integrity of public action or decision), which placed this branch of law in the context of supranational law. The second evolutionary moment is therefore accompanied by the phenomena of the *Europeanisation* and *internationalisation of* this "branch of law". Administrative law "transcends" the boundaries of state law as a result of the regulation of economic globalisation by international institutions in areas such as human rights, the environment, common natural resources, competition and international markets and foreign investment. The second half of the twentieth century was characterised by a (perhaps excessive) "administrativisation" of the economy and society.

At the moment, administrative law is facing a number of problems resulting from the economic and health crises and, even more immediately, the "return" of war to Europe. We are witnessing a strengthening of government power and a crisis in parliamentary constitutionalism, which is once again "transforming" administrative law. The current challenges increase the effectiveness of this branch of law, albeit in the context of reduced legitimisation capacity in the light of the traditional dimensions of liberal democratic constitutionalism. This is the main focus of our work.

The essential question on which this monograph is based is the following: does administrative law, as the rules and principles that govern life in society today (in a political and economic community organised according to the rules and principles of constitutional consensus), focus on the concept of material legitimacy or rather on the concept of functional authority? In other words, does administrative law imply an inalienable material dimension for the realisation of liberal social democracy, or is it sufficient for the realisation of the dominant legal-political order? Who dictates the essential content of the "idea of administrative law"—is it the legislative power or the judicial power? And another follows: Are we or are we not today facing the threat of the triumph of a "different idea" of administrative law?

1.1 A Long Road to the Autonomisation of Administrative Law as a Branch of Law

Administrative law is a *historical* and *multidisciplinary product*.

It is a *historical product* that predates the "idea of law" itself since administrative law is the product of legal institutes arising from administrative organisations that were present in the form of massive social and community organisations of the first empires.

Records relating to the "Ancient Pre-Persian and Persian Empires" (such as the Elamite, Median and Achaemenid), which occupied the plateau of present-day Iran from 6000 BC, show that even then the holders of imperial power approved rules (administrative regulations) whose aim was to organise "public" life in the community. We are referring to rules of political organisation in the form of a *state building*[2] (explaining the "federal type"—*Sasanian*—and "hierarchical" structure based on three levels of administrative division—governor, viceroy and king—as well as inter-king parity relations) and rules for managing services and infrastructures for public use (*e.g.* irrigation canals, roads and bridges, markets).

The aim of these rules was to ensure the "smooth running" of the Empire's economic and social organisation. This was ensured by a *bureaucratic organisation* based mainly on a *military organisation* and a *judicial administration*. This *judicial administration* initially applied rules from a religious source but incorporated others of a secular nature as it integrated them into the "law" seen as a cultural element of the "integrated peoples", as happened with the Babylonian Code of Hammurabi. It was a model that had the *principle of tolerance* as its founding principle (contrary to the traditional rule of conquest and subjugation), allowing this organisation to be described as *liberal* in essence. Equally important was the activity of collecting taxes and regulating them, which ensured the financing of the administrative organisation and public works and services. As an instrumental activity, the discipline of financing the administrative structure was seen as essential to its existence.

Among the countless praises that scholars give to this *Persian organisational tradition of public power*,[3] we highlight its effectiveness and efficiency in the "common" management of the complexity inherent in a territory. In fact, that social structure was already described as multicultural at the time, and for this reason, too, the territory was endowed with entities with organisational autonomy and even constituencies that were recognised as *self-governing*. This tradition also saw the creation of the concept of the *state* as an "identity referent" to which the territory, the peoples and the power of the king (sovereign) were all referred. Although power was "embodied" in a specific person, they were perceived as representing an ideal and a power that qualified them as an institution with no other parallel on earth. Records of *Persian administration and political organisation* also show the cultural and social development that those civilisations enjoyed for over 2500 years.

It is this legacy that later influenced the contributions we can draw from Ancient Greece and the Roman and Byzantine Empires to our "idea of administrative law". They added a relevant note to the Persian capacity for organisation and

---

[2] Today, the concept of *state building* is mostly associated with the "construction" of a certain model of state after the Second World War, i.e. it is used in the context of contemporary international law to designate the legal institutes and principles that must be present in the organisation or reorganisation of post-conflict political communities, which explains its association with the concept of *peacebuilding*. It is a model mostly designed by the international intuitions of the UN "universe", in which primacy is given to the establishment of a "rule of law" based on two fundamental assumptions: the separation of powers (which is inherent in the constitution of political bodies according to democratic rules) and respect for a catalogue of fundamental rights. In these ancient models what we find above all is the "idea" of organising power in the territory in order to achieve a unity of action, as well as the primacy of tolerance as an important point of social peace. Perhaps more recent reflections on the failed experience of models such as Afghanistan point to the minimalist virtues of ancient models compared to the ambition of more recent ones.

[3] Farazmand (2001), pp. 33–60.

management: the emergence of the first "answers" (science) about the nature, purpose and methods of organising life in society through *philosophy*, *ethics* and *politics*.[4]

It is at this moment and in this context that administrative law, in our opinion, is equipped with the essential elements to later become a *multidisciplinary product.*

In the period of Classical Antiquity, with the legacies of the Greek and Roman civilisations, it was possible to add to Persian efficiency and know-how some guidelines, principles or explanations about the *need for subordination to rules*. The classical philosophers spoke of "reason" (and it is here that we find the foundations of our present cultural model, a product of the Renaissance, i.e. a "return" to these values), whereby the power that regulated society had to obey rules (the idea of limiting power other than by a religious source in the strict sense of the term). And these rules stemmed from the "nature of human beings" and their behaviour, the discipline of which was essential as an element of civilisation. Human beings needed not only rules for inter-subjective relations (private law) but also rules for the "conception of how to live in society", for the "self-control" of how the rules for common life were produced and applied, *i.e.* in the political community. It is important to note that it was during this period that the principle that the *essence of public power* obeys a supra-individual objective (superior to the interests of the individual) was forged—the idea that there is a transcendence that legitimises civic duties and societal *concerns*, which opposes and overrides individual singularity. This means that the *public interest* is not measurable, negotiable or even definable by individual commitments *alone*. It is this idea that remains forever present or latent in the Western legal culture of the matrix of public law and that will mould it in the Renaissance under another rational construction, stripped of this transcendentalism,[5] although always with it in mental reserve.

In the Middle Ages, as a result of Christianity and the (re-)centralisation of power in a divine source, public law lost relevance (lost power and lost significance) due to the separation between the state and citizens and the identification of the state with divine power, with citizens only having the task of personal improvement according to the rules of the Church. Remember that in Greece and pre-Imperial

[4] It would be far beyond the scope of this work to go through all these pillars of *public law*, but we know that the training of a *jurist* presupposes reading works such as Plato's *The Republic, Nicomachean Ethics,* Aristotle's *Politics and Rhetoric* or Cicero's *De Officiis*.

[5] It is a *transcendentalism* in another form of *religiosity* (different from the one it inherited from the Persians) in which there is an intense concern with the objectives of perfecting the human being (spirit) as a way of being able to identify/dictate/create the *salus populi suprema lex,* the *supreme law that defines the collective good* (*happiness, good life*). In fact, it is this principle that is truly the *ethos of* public law, and it is to it that the dignity of the human person in its inter-relational dimension must also be reconnected. In fact, it is a truism to say that the delimitation of a space for personal self-determination in the context of life in society is the essence of the regulation of life in society, and therefore of public law.

Rome,[6] *private law* was also widespread—which explains the place that Roman law still occupies today in law teaching—but not proportionally relevant, as it was configured as a set of written rules that were applied in the activity of resolving disputes between private individuals (*ius civile*). *Public law*, on the other hand (mostly identified with the creation of the rules by which society is governed and the definition of political strategies), was elevated to an area of knowledge reserved for those who were able to work and dialogue with transcendence (philosophers, politicians and those with the gift of oratory). In the same way that it gained relevance, what we know today as *public law* has been a multidisciplinary reality since antiquity.

The theoretical path towards the autonomisation of administrative law as a branch of law in the nineteenth century gained momentum in the sixteenth century, first with the Renaissance and then with the Enlightenment. From this period, relevant contributions were made to the "origin and meaning of public law", an area in which administrative law was later autonomised. Firstly, *secularisation meant* that *sovereignty* (power) was definitively passed to a non-confessional institution, allowing the emergence of theoretical constructions of the state as not only a political entity but also a legal one. It is necessary to once again find a "reason" and "ownership' for "power".[7] Secondly, the return to classical transcendence can no longer be done according to the presuppositions of that social organisation and is adapted to the new presuppositions of *anthropocentrism*, *Renaissance humanism* and *rationalism.* This means that the origin of power in a society of equals now rests on the *contractualist theses* of Locke and Rousseau. Nevertheless, Western *public law* is still tributary to *Kantian idealism*, which ensures the link between the legitimacy of decisions and an unavailable material referent for the validity of the rules imposed. Finally, nationalisation, in the sense that all public law is built around the cultural idea of the nation state, which is the subjective universe of legitimacy and the exercise of power. The state or state community becomes the entity legitimised to define the individual's sphere of self-determination and, for this reason, it is essential to conceive and discipline the way in which this "power" acts in a clear, transparent and unequivocal manner.

It was in this sequence, and above all in the context of *nation-state law*, that *administrative law* was autonomised in the nineteenth century, again under the functional impulse or instrumental need to ensure the unity of state action in pursuit of the public interest.

It is important to note that the autonomisation of administrative law as a branch of law has been built along two distinct paths but that, today, the doctrine

[6] These assumptions changed with the creation of the Roman Empire, because at this stage, as with the Persian empires, *public law* acquired some practical relevance in terms of creating rules for the administrative organisation and distribution of power in the vast territory it encompassed. However, what emerges from the literature is that the Roman Empire was, in this respect, a step backwards, with "Romanisation" unable to follow the teachings of integrative tolerance or the organisational complexity of the Persians, which explains why Roman law is of little use in the study of administrative organisation.

[7] Loughlin (2010), pp. 37–69.

unanimously states that they have and have always had many points in common.[8] This explains the tradition of recognising legal systems in two typical models: the French continental model and the Anglo-Saxon *common law* model.

The first—the autonomisation of French continental administrative law—is based on the public authority inherent in the exercise of the executive function. Such an understanding requires an "autonomous and internal legal system" to resolve issues related to its organisation and operation, according to a centralised and hierarchical structure (with almost no room for the autonomy of local authorities), and also requires its own rules for regulating relations with private parties in order to safeguard the pursuit and primacy of the *public interest*—a right inherent to the executive function, which is the *puissance publique*[9] and which is therefore not even scrutinised by the judiciary in the light of the principle of separation of powers. We had to avoid the risk of the judiciary ending up replacing the administrative power in the exercise of this function. That is why this model requires the creation of "special bodies" with a praetorian role in defining administrative law (the *Conseil d'État* model), whose activity is still part of the administrative function, even when it begins to autonomise itself as a power to control that activity.

The second—Anglo-Saxon *common law*—is characterised by the application, as a rule, of the "same law" in relations between administrative bodies and citizens. This is mainly due to the fact that the Executive is not (constitutionally) a *power* but merely a function for executing and applying the laws (laws that limit the rights of individuals and subject them to the realisation of public interest objectives) produced by Parliament[10] and that the Government is a "parliamentary cabinet", accountable to Parliament and separate from the representative function of the State, which belongs to a neutral power, that is, the Crown. In this scheme of political organisation, inspired by the liberal model, the Public Administration is made up of a much smaller number of entities than in the French model. In the Anglo-Saxon model, the entities correspond centrally to "government departments", and to them are added the *self-government* spaces of local and corporate communities, which do not jeopardise the unity of power unified in the Crown. The Crown is the only entity with prerogatives and immunity (*the King can do no wrong*). In the *common law* model, the courts control the activity of administrative bodies,[11] ensuring the *rule of law* and the *rights of citizens*.

In fact, and as we will see in more detail in the following sections of this paper, both models for the *autonomisation of administrative law* as a *branch of law* are based on a *liberal matrix*. This matrix is then further developed in the study of the

[8] Cassese (2010), pp. 3–219.

[9] This concept, developed by Hauriou (2003) to characterise all administrative activity as power, including the provision of public services and the conclusion of contracts, is what still characterises *administrative law* today in legal systems of this cultural origin.

[10] It is true that this model provided for the possibility of *delegated legislation*, i.e. the production of legal rules by the government through an act of delegation from Parliament.

[11] This control does not prevent the recognition of *discretion* within the *judicial review of administration* and the recognition of *administrative law* within the *rule of law*.

relationship between constitutional law and administrative law, and its cornerstone is the principle of separation of powers, in particular between the judiciary and the executive or administrative power. As the doctrine today points out, the differences between these two models are not (and never have been) as real as the comparative legal method wanted to emphasise.

Thus, *administrative law*, as an autonomous branch of law, has as its "founding idea" *administrative power* or the recognition of its *functional autonomy*. Essentially, what characterizes this branch of law is the difficulty, specificity or even impossibility of controlling the merit of decisions taken with the aim of ensuring the pursuit of the *public interest*.[12] Administrative law is characterised by its *speciality* and *difference* from *private law*, and today, the differences that once deserved intense attention from the doctrine on the authoritarian or non-authoritarian origin of this difference are irrelevant at the dogmatic level, in particular the differences within the continental model between the theses that saw administrative law as a *power* (*puissance public* or *Herrschaft*) and those that saw it as a *public service* or a *functional activity.*

The *most important* thing *to retain from the idea of administrative law* as the "*DNA" of this autonomous branch of law* is its intrinsic legitimising element, which is based on values inherent to the *virtue of civility that governs the organisation and management of the economic and social superstructure*, among which, in our opinion, the most important of all is the *liberal principle*.[13] We therefore do not agree with the currents that believe that the "idea of administrative law" today is centred on the functional dimensions of guarantee, which have been highlighted in studies on the principles of proportionality, reasonableness and the protection of legitimate expectations. We have no doubt that the *essence of* administrative law is what we have stated above, and we also share the concerns of those who see in the current "threats" the risk of administrative law being distorted as a result of the *distortion of the liberal principle*.

1.2 The Relationship Between Administrative Law and Constitutional Law

As we have already mentioned, the majority doctrine has long identified *administrative law* as a by-product of *constitutional law* in the sense that it is a concretised constitutional law, along the lines of the expression coined by Werner in 1959.

---

[12] In this respect, as Cassese (2010) points out, pp. 62–66, it is a "right of privilege" or a right that derogates from private law.

[13] We are referring to the *liberalism of natural law,* which from a *political point of view* is identified with the attempt to reconcile two apparently antagonistic ideas: that men are sovereign in the governance of their political community, and that in defining the rules of that governance they are necessarily limited by a *morality that aggregates the community*—Hawley (2022), p. 224.

This interpretation of the *place and function* of administrative law in its relationship with constitutional law is particularly relevant to the exercise we have set ourselves in this monograph if we look at two essential points: the evolution of constitutional law itself and the common referent of the legitimisation of administrative law through the *democratic principle*, which underlies the *principle of legality*.

The first element we mobilise to "contest" the existence of an intrinsic relationship between administrative law and constitutional law is the fact that administrative law is an autonomous branch of law. It differs, therefore, from a mere body of organisational rules and the exercise of coercive power over citizens. The autonomy of administrative law emerged at the same time as the generalisation of elective democracy models in the mid to late twentieth century (essentially from the 1970s onwards). In fact, we have not been able to establish a meaningful connection between the advances of historic British constitutionalism and the development of *administrative law* or between French revolutionary principles and administrative law as a judicially inscrutable power or between *higher law* and US *administrative law*. It is true that there is no administrative law (just as there is no constitutional law) without the guarantee of the separation of powers and the effectiveness of fundamental rights, but it took an autonomous evolution based on jurisprudential constructions of the *principle of legality as a parameter* for *controlling discretion* for administrative law to be able to claim the status of *concretised constitutional law.*

Perhaps we should—today this idea even seems relevant to me—mobilise another meaning of concrete constitutional law and describe as *administrative law* the set of rules that govern the functioning of constitutional bodies, in particular those that hold executive power. This is a meaning, if not marginal, at least partial to the idea of administrative law that we have used as the object of study and analysis in this monograph. But it can be useful in reconstructing or making this "idea" a reality within the current dysfunctional framework of the organisation of politics and society. We will return to this theme later in this work when we begin to explore the dimensions of administrative law for the twenty-first century. For now, it is worth noting that this is not the concept of administrative law as a concretised constitutional right that the authors have been working with.

The *idea of administrative law* that informs the *concept of administrative law* is intrinsically linked to the pursuit of a model of *classical liberal democratic* values. This means that, in our way of understanding concepts and apprehending history, *administrative law is a form of political law put into effect*, not in the instrumental sense (of organising the activity of political mediators or the holders of political bodies) but in the material sense of putting the *public interest into effect*. And the public interest is conceived as the realisation of essential social values, which in themselves embody the *policy* defined in a *liberal democracy*.

The question we are studying is precisely how the *current crisis of liberal democracy* and that sense of *politics* is transmitted and reflected in *administrative law*. And the link between administrative law and constitutional law can be understood in this way, i.e. to the extent that *material constitutionalism* is also a *guarantee of liberal democracy* and not merely an instrument for legitimising formal democracies[14] where forms of *illiberalism* are growing or even a model for the development of *economic liberalism* that many point to as being responsible for the crises.

Democratic liberalism, and the *constitutionalism* that guarantees it, depends on a substrate that is characterised by a *liberal society*, something that since the twentieth century (since the emergence of contemporary constitutionalism) has been associated with the socio-political model of the United States and some European countries within the framework of the so-called Western democracies. In Europe, this idea is anchored in the European social model, and in the USA, it is based on the mutual control of powers.

The current problem is that the concept of *democratic liberalism* has lost its referent. As Fukuyama rightly emphasised in *The Origins of the Political Order*,[15] one of the great problems of democracy at the beginning of the twentieth century was not the hegemony of the concept in its merely formal sense but the (lack of) effectiveness of its axiological content. As we will see in a little more detail, most illiberal regimes were installed with irreproachable recourse to democratic elections and, in some cases, without citizens realising the context of lack of freedom in which they exercised their electoral rights.

In truth, the question that arises or should arise regarding the link between *constitutional law* and *administrative law* is not so much one of *consequent erosion*; i.e., the erosion of the nation state leads to the erosion of the normative force of the constitution, which, in turn, leads to an erosion of the "idea of administrative law" as we have presented it. Nor is it a relationship of *functional substitution*, i.e. in which the regulatory spaces that global, international and European law "expropriated" from constitutional law end up being occupied by administrative law because it is the only one with effective *enforcement* mechanisms at the level of the national legal order. The relationship between administrative law and constitutional law is a problem of *semantic-material erosion*. One of the biggest challenges facing today's societies and political-economic organisations is the *fluidity of the meaning of concepts*, which leads to principles being interpreted so widely that their effectiveness is compromised. It is precisely in order to reintegrate the meaning of concepts and the importance of institutions that a return to the classics is relevant.

At this point, what we describe as a *crisis of the idea of administrative law* coincides with what Loughlin identifies as the crisis of liberal democratic constitutionalism.[16] Apparently, we would be arguing the opposite of Loughlin since the author is against the concept of constitutionalism of the mid-twentieth century (the

[14] This is one of the great challenges of so called *state-building*, which international institutions like the UN take on as their own task or programme, wrapped up in theories that they then try to implement in practice, but which often fail because they don't "inspire" and "incorporate" the ethics of the local community. There have been successive studies on the failures of these programmes in various regions of the world, with the case of the Arab Spring—Erdogan (2021) being particularly relevant in this context for Europeans.

[15] Fukuyama (2011).

[16] Loughlin (2022), pp. 191–202. Similarly, Fukuyama (2022).

constitutionalism of the modern phase) based on legal principles and the guarantee of fundamental rights. In his view, this understanding of constitutionalism has unbalanced the powers in favour of the judiciary and transformed the *theory of limited government*, which maximised the democratic principle, into a *constitutionalism of abstract and universal principles with non-democratic roots*[17] while at the same time *transmuting the legislative power* into a mere executor of constitutional values and principles. For Loughlin, these material principles that restrict and distort democratic power, imposing the "rational discourse of rights" under the alleged aim of defending the individual, have destroyed all the collective organisational and institutional elements, from hierarchy to the bureaucratic rules that discipline collective decisions, culminating in the fragmentation of the boundaries between public and private. According to the author, this individualist constitutionalism, which opposed the guarantees provided by institutions, which expanded which expanded the universal principles of law (in themselves without any content of their own, such as proportionality, reasonableness or equality) as a promotion of rights and individual well-being, and which blurred the boundaries between the national and the international, resulted in a form of destruction of liberal democracies. Now, by proposing that administrative law should not be a mere functional instrument and should be geared towards the realisation of the *public interest*, which inescapably includes elements relating to community life, we are meeting the same idea that underlies Loughlin's thesis[18] and we are agreeing with the idea that *liberal democracy* cannot be reduced to a normative concept and, even less so, to a question of law that can be controlled or guaranteed through the courts. Constitutional democracy must remain an expression of liberalism, ensuring a balance between collective freedom (which is characterised by duties) and individual autonomy.

Our proposal is in line with the author's in recognising that only the activity of political and social institutions within the framework of constitutional democracy can make it possible to fulfil the aims of individual freedom (diversity of thought) and social (fair income) and cultural (tolerance) well-being, both in defining public policies within the framework of a liberal democratic rule of law and in defining how they are implemented within the framework of administrative law that allows

[17] Levinson (2006).

[18] The author lists six perversions of the constitutionalism of rights in the (re)formulation of the Constitution: *i)* as a framework for understanding society (instead of being limited to a framework for understanding government or power); *ii)* as a symbol of representation of collective political identity (instead of being only a representation of government); *iii)* the horizontal division of powers that limited the Executive, becomes a vertical scheme of differentiation of powers in the global, regional, national and local arenas; *iv) it* ceases to be a legitimising framework for government and becomes the constitutionalisation of intergovernmental arrangements; *v)* fundamental law becomes the written expression of universal public reason; and *vi)* what was a statute for the regime of collective political identity becomes a form of neoliberal values with global reach—Loughlin (2022), p. 195.

the public interest to be achieved.[19] As Krastev and Holmes propose, it is necessary to re-found *classical liberalism once again.*[20]

1.3 The "New" Administrative Law of the Twentieth Century

The late twentieth and early twenty-first centuries were characterised by the emergence of the *new administrative law*, which coincides with the emergence of the "constitutionalism of rights". The term was coined mainly with the publication of the German treatise organised by Professors Hoffmann-Riem, Schmidt-Aßmann and Voßkuhle (first edition 2006). Some 20 years on from this publication and bearing in mind the significant changes that have taken place in the meantime, both on a societal level and on a legal-political and economic level, it seems right to conclude that this *new administrative law*, like the criticisms that can be levelled at the constitutionalism of rights, has not been able to solve many of the problems that today affect the daily lives of citizens in Western countries. What is more, the achievements in terms of well-being[21] and security[22] that liberal capitalism of the mid-twentieth century brought about are once again being called into question.

This landmark work on administrative law (not just for German doctrine but also for all Europeans) revisits the main topics of this branch of law under an intense theoretical reflection that places special emphasis on the legal control of administrative activity and the *functional dimension of* law, in particular economic analysis, cost-benefit analysis and behavioural analysis in general as an instrument for modelling behaviour and economic regulation.[23] Despite the differences in style between the chapters, the book aims to highlight some points that, in the opinion of the organisers, constitute a different dimension of administrative law, which breaks with traditional issues.

---

[19] In the re-reading that everyone is currently doing of authors who have been a reference in the construction of public law and administrative law, we would also highlight the study dedicated to the thought of Ernst-Wolfgang Böckenförde, for whom the liberal democratic state had an essential role, subsidiary to that of society and the market economy, in guaranteeing social rights, restoring essential balances to peace, which was an inherent value of community life Böckenförde (2017).

[20] Krastev and Holmes (2019), p. 30.

[21] The latest figures show that the "1% phenomenon" (1% of the population concentrates the world's wealth produced by everyone else) and the worsening of inequalities, highlighted by Stiglitz (2012) among others, has continued to grow this century.

[22] The threat to peace after the Second World War became an endemic phenomenon with the counter-terrorism policy that began after 11 September, and it has constantly worsened. With the outbreak of the war in Ukraine, Europe is witnessing a succession of threats to peace, be it economic, financial, energy, food or political, with a permanent endeavour to show a European Union with very significant internal divisions.

[23] Thaler and Sunstein (2008).

Thus, instead of being centred on the area of valuation of administrative power, which is un-scrutinisable by the judiciary (the issues of discretion and indeterminate concepts), the "new administrative law" takes on a *functional* nature, linked to the exercise of a task of *regulation* and management of the public interest, which is no longer entrusted only to administrative entities but can also be exercised by private individuals and entities independent of the executive power, but all subject to judicial control. At the same time as analysing this broadening of scope, there is a "narrowing" of *discretion*, with the need to ensure legal control guided by the new principles of the "ordering idea of administrative law",[24] with particular emphasis on proportionality, equality, legal certainty, sustainability and reasonableness. The result is a very eclectic administrative law with ductile characteristics, which expands its powers of regulation in competition with (and in addition to) the power of the legislator, which acts in new and variable ways using the objectives of economic science and the tools of behavioural social sciences (sociology, psychology and management). Administrative law is also colonising different areas, particularly sanctions law,[25] while at the same time no longer claiming differences in traditional topics such as public employment or public services.

Administrative law, thus de-characterised from the distinctive marks that led to its autonomy as a branch of law—the power to implement the public interest—is in fact the product of transformations in public (de-)intervention in the economic

[24] We are referring to Schmidt-Assmann's proposal for a "recomprehension" of the idea of general administrative law associated with its subordination to fundamental rights, the law and legal principles (juridicity) and the judicial scrutiny of all acts from this general perspective of concretised constitutional law—Schmidt-Assmann (1998).

[25] We believe that the *administrativisation of sanctions law* is particularly disruptive to the essence of administrative law, as it calls into question the traditional boundaries between criminal law, where the guarantees of citizens must necessarily prevail, and administrative law, where the functional power of the state to achieve the public interest must prevail. By retracting the importance of administrative power in the organisation and operation of economic activities that are relevant to life in society and associating the guarantee of the public interest with the power to sanction private individuals, the problem arises of which dimension takes precedence. In addition, economic sanctions (especially regulatory sanctions) applied by administrative authorities to whom the power to regulate markets has been delegated are particularly severe, reaching amounts much higher than those of a fine, which makes it unreasonable, from this point of view, not to apply the guarantees of criminal law. However, on the other hand, these guarantees are out of step with the type and nature of the administrative sanction. In our view, the power to prosecute and punish those who commit a crime cannot be confused with the power to penalise those who flout market economy rules; there is no identity in the values that are violated or in the disvalue that is associated with them. But the tendency has been the opposite, that is, to approach and even overvalue infringements of market rules, considering that they also result in an infringement of values present in the "social pact".

area[26] and the growing autonomy of radical individualist fundamental rights. It is the state *regulating* private and (re-)privatised economic activity—which, in Europe, corresponds to an *import and adaptation of the North American idea of regulation*, complemented with the values dictated by the post-war European legal heritage, centred on guaranteeing the fundamental rights—and the *guarantor state*—of a citizen protected in their individualism (and selfishness) in an ever-increasing number of legal spheres—which provide the fertile ground for the "perversion" of the meaning of "new administrative law", the idea of which is ultimately determinable by a judicial body.

Added to this, in the context of the flourishing—with economic globalisation and the various meanings of integration (economic, political and social)—of supranational bureaucratic structures, based on inter-governability agreements, is a further expansion of this branch of law. Both for the discipline of organisational issues and for the discipline of functional aspects of these new spheres of *regulation*, which are intertwined with national production rules and private normative production—phenomena that characterise the erosion of the principle of legality—administrative law acquires yet another perversion of meaning.

The expansive wave of administrative law highlights not only its many weaknesses and shortcomings as a judicially determinable "ordering legal idea", but above all the risks of an administrative state dissociated from a legitimisation based on liberal democratic institutions.

It is interesting to note that the authors agree on the assumption that administrative law must give concrete expression to a supra-legal value or values, but they differ as to whether or not they are identified with the legal principles and fundamental rights of post-war constitutionalism and globalisation. The authors also agree on the need to ensure the effectiveness of these values through administrative activity or activity subject to administrative activity, but they differ on how this should be ensured as some support the primacy of judicial control with the ability to define these values and others prefer to place the emphasis on the production of administrative law by democratic means and on control through the institutionalisation of administrative activity.

1.4 The Crossroads of Administrative Law in the Twenty-First Century

The first misconception that becomes clear is that *administrative law* is inseparable from *constitutional law* as the regulatory law of liberal democratic institutions, and we believe that today, it is difficult to defend the *autonomy of administrative law*

[26] The *new administrative law* is part of the *narrative on the evolution of the role of the state in the economy* with the transition from the liberal state to the social state and from there to the regulatory and guarantee state. In this *narrative* about the functions of the state, the relationship between the state and the economy is given primacy, and the following moments are matched.

and its *jurisprudential* force in isolation from a democratic and liberal institutional framework. Administrative law is a *regulatory tool*, it is capable of supporting decisions of power, but it is not capable of generating *law*. It is capable of *guaranteeing rights* within the framework of the public interest but not of supporting solutions that superimpose citizens' rights on the public interest on the basis of *law not dictated by democratic rules*.

We agree—again—with Loughlin when he warns that Bobbio was right when he warned that *legitimate law* had to be a product of a liberal democratic state, i.e. a state in which decisions were adopted in a democratic and "controllable" way and that when there was an increase in "opacity in normative production", there was also a corresponding reduction in the legitimacy of these rules.[27] The constitutionalism of rights and the *new administrative law* tried to make up for the organisational complexity and regulatory production, which was necessarily less democratic, with *legitimacy through ends*, through the promotion of legitimate ends. But the issue being debated today is that this path, being less democratic, is less legitimate, not only because it disregards the principles of liberalism, but also in terms of the results it produces.

In essence, an *administrative law that utilises trump cards against majorities* can be, as we shall see, an *instrument for promoting illiberalism* and the *tyranny of minorities*.[28]

The first example of this assumption is the *2008 financial crisis*. After the fall of the Berlin Wall, Europe and the world put their faith in lasting peace and turned to the implementation of liberal capitalism, believing that state intervention should be reduced to the aforementioned regulatory and guarantee functions. But the result of this economic and social model (based on the premises of privatisation, economic self-regulation and an open society), which the West, through the institutions of global governance (especially the UN institutional system), wanted to expand and impose in the context of *state-building* policies, *turned out* to be misguided, if not self-flagellating, perhaps because of the arrogance of claiming to be the "only model of development" and certainly because it was based on a "perversion and corruption" of the basic concept: that of *classical liberalism*.

Contrary to the Western narrative, in other areas of the world, alternative socio-economic development models to liberal capitalism have been developed and have borne fruit. At the same time, liberal capitalism in the West was giving way to a profound increase in inequality, and the *sub-prime crisis* showed the dangers of financial deregulation and the injustices it can lead to and generalised a feeling of discredit in politics and democratic institutions. On this occasion, it was concluded that *economic freedoms were* not functionalised for the common good, that economic *utilitarianism* was unethical, that the *social responsibility of private individuals* was a decoy and that society had been deceived by the market economy. The crisis of confidence that has arisen is not one of the markets but of society in the face

[27] Loughlin (2022).

[28] Levitsky and Ziblatt (2023).

of the institutions of the free market and its alleged instruments of control, including the states, which have proved ineffective in managing these problems.

The second example is identifiable from the huge discussion around the *administrative states of emergency* determined in the context of managing the COVID-19 pandemic. Many governments around the world, faced with the risk (scientific uncertainty about the disease caused by the virus) and the lack of means (to prevent contagion and treat symptoms), adopted measures to restrict contact between the population, with particular emphasis on confinement, i.e. imposing rules and bans on movement. The adoption of these measures, which in European countries has not been the subject of significant social protest, in the sense of leading to the adoption of strong police measures or the containment of a threat of civil disobedience, has nevertheless been challenged in court in almost all states, citing the violation of fundamental rights and the legitimacy of their adoption.

It is interesting to note that most of the court judgements ruled not on the *proportionality* or *necessity of* the specific confinement measures but rather on the legitimacy of their adoption (with most of them ruling that it was a measure restricting fundamental rights that could only be approved by Parliament) and on the conditions for approving states of constitutional emergency.[29]

In this specific case, the courts treated the issue as a restriction of fundamental rights—considering that the issue was not reducible to the rules for managing public health problems and, as such, to administrative measures for regulating behaviour, resurrecting, in some cases, problems that were thought to have already been overcome by scientific and social consensus, such as compulsory vaccination—and invoked the premises of democratic liberalism—the need for parliamentary intervention—stating or implying that administrative power was insufficient for the intensity or seriousness of the measures adopted—in order to basically agree with the theses that populist and illiberal movements had put forward in the public arena. The most striking thing about what has been written on this subject is the way in which the loss of material significance of political and normative institutes enables and enhances these perverted results. The mere intervention of parliaments turned out to be what the case law analysed (and the lack of which it condemned) and what the doctrine called for, apparently ignoring what had already been discussed about the risks of the constitutional state of exception in the episodes of the US reaction to the September 11 attacks.

In this episode of democratic collective life, legitimisation based on mere exercises of form has been demanded, as is the case in the growing illiberal democracies with periodic elections, which for this reason alone have to be described as democratic.

At this point, there is a clear lack of *material* democratic legitimacy or, to put it more precisely, the mere formal democratic legitimacy of much of the *administrative law* that is applied daily in the courts, where the control parameters do not rest on democratically defined solutions for reconciling individual rights with the public

[29] Barnés (2021), pp. 101–193; Agamben (2015).

interest. This is compounded by the de-legitimisation of decisions in which the courts do not even apply normative parameters formally dictated by democratic power and limit themselves to *imitating* solutions dictated by institutions without direct democratic legitimacy (as is the case with transposing European case law from the ECtHR or the CJEU) or extracting from fundamental principles or principle-rules that set out the rights of the individual, solutions that they attribute to the law but that are their own creation, or, worse still, to invoke rules protecting community values in order to extract solutions of individual advantage from them against the other holders of the same legal good. This is a *growing illiberal administrative law* dictated under the auspices of guaranteeing the promotion of the liberal development model.

And we are witnessing a second misunderstanding of the expansion of so-called autonomous administrative law and yet another expression of its *illiberal* nature in order to respond to the challenges of today's society. We are referring to the regulation of *economic and social digitalisation* and the *expansion of the use of weak artificial intelligence tools* in various administrative procedures, including behavioural regulation.

In the case of the *digitalisation of administrative information*, which then leads to the electronic processing of procedures and the practice of administrative acts *in* electronic *form*, the threats are only characterised by the lack of a decision based on human rationality and its inalienable weighting, something that Article 22 of the European Data Protection Regulation (Regulation (EU) 2016/679) prohibits. Article 22 of the European Data Protection Regulation (Regulation (EU) 2016/679) prohibits this by enshrining the (European) right not to be subject to decisions based exclusively on automated means when the decision produces legal effects concerning the person or significantly affects them (e.g. access to social rights or even a bank loan).

On the other hand, the widespread use of *weak artificial intelligence tools*, i.e. behaviours or solutions determined by algorithms, lacks strong and effective counter-analysis tools, especially to neutralise the effects of *bias*, which, being common in the way humans react to certain stimuli or ideas, end up being transmitted to algorithms, without this transmission process being fully known and easy to correct. The issue lies in the relevance of the rationale to the solution since the algorithm is, as a rule, non-transparent and the decision that affects the person must be rationally supported.

Thus, *procedural automation* and *artificial intelligence (AI)* are tools that assist in administrative tasks, but they cannot be autonomous forms of decision-making, nor can they contribute to the autonomisation of administrative law, nor even to the expansion of administrative valuation spaces (they cannot be a source of discretion) or even to support decisions based on technical criteria.

It is in this context that a relevant area of the juridicisation of AI and automation has been developing, where the idea of banning algorithms as black boxes for administrative decisions stands out.

References

Agamben G (2015) State of exception (trans: Attell K). University of Chicago Press, Chicago

Barnés J (2021) The crisis of parliamentary democracy. The case of COVID-19. RAP 216:101–139

Böckenförde EW (2017) In: Kunkler M, Stein T (eds) Constitutional and political theory. Selected writings. Oxford University Press, Croydon

Cassese S (2010) Il diritto amministrativo: Storia e Prospettive. Giuffrè Editore, Milano

Erdogan A (2021) Arab Spring - Arab Fall. Divergent transitions in post-2011 Tunisia and Egypt. Lexington Books, Lanham

Farazmand A (2001) Learning from Ancient Persia: administration of the Persian Achamenid World-State Empire. In: Farazmand A (ed) Handbook of comparative and development public administration. Marcel Dekker, New York

Fukuyama F (2011) The origins of the political order: from prehuman times to the French revolution. Farrar, Straus and Giroux, New York

Fukuyama F (2022) Liberalism and its discontents. Profile Books, London

Ginsburg T (2017) Written constitutions and the administrative state: on the constitutional character of administrative law. In: Rose-Ackerman S et al (eds) Comparative administrative law. Edward Elgar, Cheltenham

Hauriou M (2003) Principios de derecho público y constitucional (trans: del Castillo CR). Comares, Granada

Hawley M (2022) Natural law republicanism. Cicero's liberal legacy. Oxford University Press, New York

Krastev I, Holmes S (2019) The light that failed. A reckoning. Penguin Books, London

Levinson S (2006) Our undemocratic constitution. Where the constitution goes wrong (and how we the people can correct it). Oxford University Press, Oxford

Levitsky S, Ziblatt D (2023) Tyranny of the minority. Crown, New York

Loughlin M (2010) Foundations of public law. Oxford University Press, New York

Loughlin M (2022) Agaisnt constitutionalism. Harvard University Press, Cambridge

Schmidt-Assmann E (1998) Das allgemeine Verwaltungsrecht als Ordnungsidee. Grundlagen und Aufgaben der verwaltungsrechtlichen Systembildung. Springer, Berlin

Stiglitz J (2012) The price of inequality. W. W. Norton & Company, New York

Thaler R, Sunstein C (2008) Nudge: improving decisions about health, wealth, and happiness. Yale University Press

Wollenschläger F (2017) Constitutionalisation and deconstitutionalisation of administrative law in view of Europeanisation and emancipation. REAL 1:7–79

Chapter 2
The Theoretical and Legal-Institutional Context

The "idea of administrative law" that we present and defend here is derived from a model of *administrative law from the liberal state*, so it is important to start by clearly identifying for our reader the "theoretical code" that underlies our dialogical construction and that, as we shall see, is far removed from what we describe as a "conceptual adulteration" that was introduced at the end of the last century and the beginning of this century.

In this part, we will "dialogue" with the theory, essentially on the basis of four works: *Liberalism and Its Discontents* by Francis Fukuyama (2022); *The Light That Goes Out. How the West Won the Cold War but Lost the Peace* by Ivan Krastev and Stephen Holmes (2019); *Power to the People. Constitutionalism in the Age of Populism* by Mark Tushnet and Bojan Bugaric (2021); and *The Constitution of the Common Good* by Adrian Vermeule (2022).

It should be remembered that the concept of *liberalism we are* starting from is the one that began to be forged in the seventeenth century with the end of the wars of religion in Europe (or, as many prefer to call it, after the Peace of Westphalia) and that obtained the generalised consensus of the doctrine based on the essential premises of the need for the state (contractualist theses[1]) as a guarantor of peace and the common good (of everyone's rights), democracy as an instrument for legitimising power and individualism as a guarantee of dignity in the dimension of the right to personal self-determination.

[1] It is not our aim here to transcribe the summary of the works of the "contractualists", but only to point out that they all ended up "justifying" the need for the state, as a political order or authority, as a way of ultimately guaranteeing individual rights, whether it was to "neutralise" the predatory power of individuals over others (in Hobbes' conception), or to guarantee original equality (in Rousseau's version), or to ensure property rights and freedom of economic self-determination and the neutralisation of tyrannical power (in Locke's version).

S. Tavares da Silva, *Administrative Law for the 21st Century*,
https://doi.org/10.1007/978-3-031-55795-8_2

2.1 The "Crisis" of Democratic Liberalism and the Emergence of Illiberalism

The concept of *liberalism* outlined above occupies a central place in our construction, as does the rejection of the "abuses", "deviations" or "excesses" to which the concept of classical liberalism was subjected and that culminated in its crisis.

Fukuyama's considerations (2022) are significant in this regard. The author presents three justifications for the promotion of *liberal societies*: a *pragmatic rational one*, in that liberalism is a guarantor of peace (as the classical tradition has already shown); a *moral one*, because liberalism is the only one that can defend the autonomy of the individual; and an *economic* one, because economic history shows that the liberal principles of promoting private property and freedom of trade are at the root of economic growth. As we said about antiquity, Fukuyama also emphasises that the concept of *liberalism* aims to respond to a problem of governance over diversity (over plural societies, whether in religious, racial or ethnic terms, etc.) and that the founding principle of this theory is *tolerance*, imposing a fundamental difference between private life (governed by self-determination) and public life in which essential limitations prevail to guarantee peace in life in society.

Classical liberalism, in itself already a tributary of the *liberalism of antiquity*, restored as an essential theory of the organisation of public and political power at the end of the seventeenth century and widely cultivated in the eighteenth century (with the tributes of the Enlightenment philosophy), is once again postponed at the beginning of the twentieth century with the expansion of nationalist and communist theories: the former through national (and racial, in the Nazi case) identity politics, which destroyed individualism, and the latter through the rejection of private property and free trade.

It was then that we once again saw a re-founding of liberal principles, firstly, in the post-World War II period, with the creation in Europe of models of judicialised constitutionalism[2] and the foundation of a new international order based on these principles and guaranteed by the UN system and financed by the World Bank, as well as other supra-state political systems (also progressively juridicised and judicialised), particularly in Europe,[3,4] and, secondly, with the "fall of the Berlin Wall"

[2] We are referring to the constitution of constitutional states in which the essential rules of classical liberalism are elevated to fundamental legal rules and their guarantee is entrusted to organs of the judiciary, with the emergence of a special type of court such as the "German-style constitutional courts".

[3] We are referring to the Council of Europe system, the European Union and the supranational courts—such as the ECHR and the CJEU—which are progressively demanding areas of action and *enforcement of* their decisions through the actions of their respective courts.

[4] This model of political, economic and social organisation has had and still has aspirations to expand to other areas of the globe, but for various reasons that we are unable to analyse here (from historical-cultural to ethno-demographic) it has not been able to be implemented beyond mere commercial arrangements when there are conditions of mutual gain, i.e. without it being possible to "build" supranational models there based on moral values or principles. The most flagrant case of failure is the system of the Inter-American Commission on Human Rights and its Court based in Costa Rica.

and Deng Xiaoping's reforms and the transition of Eastern European and Asian economies to market regimes, with the corresponding "entry" into the world trade system.

But these principles are once again threatened by "excesses", "setbacks" and "misrepresentations" of their useful and ultimate meaning.

Firstly, on the economic front, liberalism is "distorted" by the economic school of "neoliberalism" based on the contributions of the laureate economists of the "Chicago School" and the "Austrian School",[5] who developed a theory, *roughly speaking*, based exclusively on the virtues of free markets and their capacity for self-management and self-regulation based on consumption and its indicators (prices and quality), blaming state intervention in this area for dis-economies and obstacles to development, first economic and then social. They are at the root of various political-administrative reforms that began in the 1990s found on on the alleged need to *reduce* the state and *privatise economic areas and sectors.*

This is a kind of *economic libertarianism* that many believe was at the root of the financial crises of 2008 and 2010, which had their origins precisely in the excessive financial risk taken by investment banks and proved their inability to self-regulate. In fact, the problem now shows that the pernicious effects of deregulating or self-regulating the economy are not confined to the financial markets. The years of "trust" in the markets have led to major entropies in economic redistribution and to an accumulation of wealth in small groups that leads to results completely opposite to those on which classical liberalism is based. This economic entropy, which dismantles liberal society and once again undermines peace, continues under a discourse that is in itself evidence of the problem: while the defenders of *economic libertarianism* claim the liberal matrix as the foundation of their behaviour and present macroeconomic results as indicators of success, the critics reveal the data of increasing social inequalities, claim that aggregate wealth is not and cannot be synonymous with economic development and call for a return to classical liberal principles. This *new reform*, based once again on recovering the principles of *classical liberalism* and putting an end to the idea that all well-being can be measured on the basis of consumption indices, has adopted the name of a *fair economic model*, which seeks to reconcile economic well-being with labour dignity, the preservation of scarce natural resources and the safeguarding of cultural values. As Fukuyama rightly states: "there is no reason why economic efficiency should 'triumph' over all other social values".

In the meantime, the social drama imposed by the succession of economic crises—prompted by the financial crisis of 2008, the sovereign debt crisis of European

---

[5] To mention just a few representatives of this "ideological current", we have Milton Friedman (Nobel Prize winner in 1976) and his work on "the study of consumer behaviour" and his contributions to monetary stabilisation policies (which represented an "overcoming" of Keynesian proposals for state intervention); George Stigler (Nobel in 1982) and his work on the role of information in the economy, which is very relevant to regulating competition; and Friedrich Hayek (Nobel in 1974) and his work on the relevant and positive role of free markets in innovation, wealth creation and the transmission of price signals.

countries in 2010, COVID in 2019 and the Ukrainian War in 2021, to which must be added the "non-transparent" crisis of the mass reception of migrants since 2009—has led to the adoption of welfare policies, especially in Europe, which undermine the environment of freedom and "trust" that must govern the proper functioning of the democratic system of a liberal state.

Secondly, we point to *narcissistic individualism* as the second excess incurred by the liberal model (re-)founded in the second half of the twentieth century. The return of social regulation to the economic individual who is exclusively concerned (and occupied) with maximising economic well-being, which is the origin of the transposition of the "game theory" into various areas of social relations, has obscured the importance of other essential aspects that govern social relations and whose indirect regulation is also fundamental to ensuring peace. In fact, the principle of *classical liberalism is* based precisely on the protection of the free space for personal self-determination and the protection of a space for collective self-determination to democratically set the rules on which personal self-determination is formed.

As Fukuyama explains, in their lifelong learning, individuals are guaranteed the power of self-determination or choice, which they exercise within the framework of the legal, civic and cultural rules laid down by the political community in which they belong, and they also enjoy the freedom, within the framework of the rules that organise that political community, to be able to participate in defining those rules together with others and within the framework of the "free market of ideas" and according to the democratic principle. However, since the second half of the last century, we have also seen a disruption of these postulates, refuting the *legitimacy of the democratic game* to define the rules under which individual choices are made.

In this respect, many authors today point to the construction of John Rawls' theory of justice[6] as the *source* of the disruption. Let us remember that Rawls presented himself as a *liberal* who, like Kant, considers man to be a free being, capable of producing the rules on which to base his choice of life, which is the *ultimate freedom*. However, he rejects *Kant's idea* of the *categorical imperative* and the relegation of justice—the value that presides over the choice of the rule that regulates the choice—to something transhuman and relegates this value back to the individual, believing that he is capable of making just choices in the "original position" or "under the veil of ignorance". He therefore rejects the idea that individuals can be treated differently depending on their choices.

There are many critics of this construction of justice, or of the popular use that may have been made of it.[7] We are particularly interested in "swelling these ranks" from the position of those who believe that Rwals' construction of justice is a misrepresentation—yet another—of *classical liberalism*, emphasising the idea that not all individual choices can be neutral on a social level and that, therefore, not all of them can be disregarded on the ground that everything constitutes pernicious social oppression.

[6] The critique covers both the original version of Rawls' theory of justice (1971) and the revised version (1999).

[7] We have intentionally left an opening to welcome the thoughtful arguments of authors who believe that part of this interpretation is attributable to the adulteration of Rawls' thought.

It is precisely the generalisation or vulgarisation of the rejection of any form of so-called social oppression that is at the root of *identity politics* and group social movements. Legal institutes that emerged as positive proposals in the field of equality and human dignity have also ended up being captured and degenerated by identity politics. This is the case with affirmative actions or Dworkin's proposal to understand fundamental rights as the trump cards of minorities. The principle of classical liberalism that individual freedom must be exercised within the framework of a consensus on the space for exercising these freedoms, which is defined by democratic rules, has been completely postponed. The thesis that social consensus is liberal and not oppressive, because it peacefully allows everyone to have room for personal self-determination without affecting social unity, has been groundlessly rejected. What is more, the individual's real context is social and group, and even their self-determination is relational, so it is essential that the rules of this space for self-determination include contextual elements that contribute to social peace.

Finally, we also follow Fukuyama's concern about the "rejection" of scientific rationalism and its replacement by the "excesses" of theories based on "radical subjectivity", more specifically the risks of Derrida's deconstructionist theories, Saussure's post-modernist theories or Foucault's biopower theories, all of which share a rejection of the "narrative" of modern liberalism, disruptive proposals that destroy codes of communication and consensual scientific methods, paving the way for the "government of fear", "permanent uncertainty" and the countless conspiratorial narratives that undermine collective (and also individual) life in a democratic society—dangers that, added to the policing of public discourse and the manipulation of social networks, take the centrality of true personal freedom away, replacing it with a tribalised, digitally manipulated and frightened society.

That is why Fukuyama is also calling for a new moment of re-founding the principles of classical democratic liberalism based on the principle of tolerance to overcome the excesses of the progressive left; the subordination of the economy to rules that prioritise the social interest, in particular the redistribution of income; the improvement of the quality of government; the promotion of freedom of expression; and the guarantee of individual rights to self-determination within the framework of the limitations inherent in guaranteeing a good life.

2.2 The Emergence of Authoritarian and Hybrid Constitutionalism

Another work that marks the most current reflections on the decline and need for change in the Western model of the state and social and economic organisation is Ivan Krastev and Stephen Holmes' book, *The Fading Light*. In this book, the authors essentially look at the reasons for the emergence of *illiberalism* in European countries such as Hungary and Poland. They conclude that it is essentially a "reaction" to the dominant Western methodology and a way of expressing an identity of its own, in reaction to the domination of *copycat Westernisation*, which followed communist rule.

The authors also start from the post-Cold War context and consider that the failure of the communist economic model gave rise to a generalised imitation of the Western model of democratic liberalism but with different nuances: a model of *imitation of the means* or *appropriation*, which was adopted by China very skilfully as it managed to obtain the transfer of technology they needed to modernise their economy, have access to markets to export their goods and ensure economic growth while at the same time neutralising the "adulteration" of their cultural matrix; a model of *imitation of ends* or *conversion*, which includes the Eastern European countries, which believed that imitating Western values and models would be a path to development; and a model of *imitation of appearances* or *simulation*, which was adopted by the Russian elites in an apparent way only to allow access to the open-world economy while, internally, maintaining the structure of privileges and thus managing to build a powerful oligarchic system. In this context, the authors believe that *Western democratic liberalism* ended up losing the greatest of its conquests: peace.

Indeed, from Eastern Europe come strong reactions from members of the system—the so-called converts—who do not accept the rules and adopt illiberal measures (calling into question the independence of the courts in judging questions of public law or repealing or not applying in their own jurisdictions rules dictated by the European Union in alleged fulfilment of European values of liberalism, as is the case with rules on immigration law), legitimising their adoption through democratic expedients, which Europe claims are only formally democratic. From Russia comes the end of the simulation of adherence to democratic rules and an armed response to the attempt to expand the liberal ideology to countries in the former bloc, as with Ukraine. And from China comes a new global economic hegemony, backed by an emerging economy that proposes to "help" financially those countries that want it without imposing conditions on political, legal or social organisations while at the same time internally intensely controlling the possibility of any "adulteration" of the Chinese model with Western values. The authors emphasise that Western societies have not shown leadership in the face of these "global threats" to the expansion of illiberalism, nor have they managed to improve the model's external image after the 2008 financial crisis.

It is important to remember that Stephen Holmes is a scholar of the crisis of classical liberalism and anti-liberal currents and that in his most recent writings,[8] he considers that the "antipathy" towards liberalism that is present in current trends, although nothing new, should merit our concern because it jeopardises the international order that we built after the Second World War and represents a global threat to the values of peace and freedom. These movements are characterised by systematically pointing out the defects and shortcomings of liberalism, which they identify with the "atomisation of the individual" and the destruction of societal and community ties, transforming society into a collection of selfish, self-centred individuals devoid of moral values. The author counters that the liberal conception of the individual does not ignore their *social ethos* but is based on the dogma that none of

[8] Holmes (2022), pp. 3ff.

their affiliations (family, political, racial, economic, social, religious, etc.) can neutralise their individuality because in this set of "belongings" to which each person is tributary, the level of involvement is self-determined, i.e. the subject is always self-conforming and can never be reduced to a mere member of a group. This also means that the rule is not group loyalty but self-determination, without prejudice to the fact that some present social currents seek precisely to rebuild forms of "social tribalism" through social networks, which constitutes a threat to liberal values. It is also common for anti-liberals to point to liberalism as an "ideology of the rich", insofar as the freedom of choice and self-determination they proclaim is only real for those who have the material conditions to be able to exercise it, which is not the case for the majority of the population whose income is captured by economic and financial deregulation.

Liberalism is, like all ideologies, more perfect in its formulation than in its execution, and, as Holmes rightly points out, there is an embarrassing side to the cult of liberalism when you realise that the "heroic moments" of history were not those guided by the ideals of tolerance, peace and political stability but rather those in which slave labour dominated (as in the construction of the pyramids), colonialism and imperialism (which made it possible to fill European museums with works and testimonies from other cultures and to build monuments symbolising domination) or even man's "unregulated" interference in nature or in the use of science (which makes it possible to fear human action in areas such as genetics or nuclear energy and, more recently, artificial intelligence). Despite this, these are not (or should not be) reasons to cultivate illiberalism or even to reject the many virtues of its classic formulation.

In a different vein, Mark Tushnet and Bojan Bugaric analyse the phenomenon of populism, which most authors associate with illiberalism but which they decide to critically analyse from another perspective: whether populism is totally incompatible with constitutionalism. For the purpose of our reflection, this is a particularly interesting perspective of analysis since it provides new insights into the role of judicial control in the defence or otherwise of the liberal democratic model.

For Tushnet and Bugaric, "constitutionalism" should mostly be reduced to four characterising elements: majority rule, the existence of a system of political parties, the independence of the judiciary and the immutability of institutions and certain policies by mere "majority rule". And contrary to most of the doctrine, these authors consider that *populism* is not necessarily incompatible with these dimensions, including the constitutional and institutional reforms that many "populist political movements" propose and that may even be necessary to overcome the "deadlocks" ("permanent veto" regimes) in which many Western political systems find themselves. From an overall perspective, the authors' proposal is that there is a "positive dimension" to *populism* in that it presents itself as a way, often reconcilable with *mainstream* political actors, to "unblock" the functioning of liberal democracies and make it possible to carry out the reforms that the current constitutional systems seem to be preventing.

Interpreted in this way, the authors' proposal ends up meeting solutions that other authors also consider essential in the context of guaranteeing liberal democracies, although they understand that these solutions need to be built on other theoretical foundations.

This is the case with Martin Loughlin, for whom the current problem with the healthy functioning of liberal democracies is precisely the result of *constitutionalism* and its *philosophy of limiting power by limiting government*, which the author calls "civil religion", imposing unnecessary difficulties on today's societies in solving their problems by "neutralising" majority rule and preventing institutional reforms. Loughlin believes that the current problem of liberal democracies lies in the fact that there has been an internal "quasi-balkanisation" within national states as a result of globalisation, which has led to countries acquiring an economic and social structure that divides the big cities and their populations, linked to each other by these international economic flows (tourism, company headquarters, transport facilities), from the rural part of the country, where jobs are scarce, pay is lower and isolation is rife due to poor access to services. The population is divided into two distinct groups, and from this emerges the dynamic of "confrontation" that characterises populism between the cosmopolitan and the rural. And the *constitutionalism of the first half of the twentieth century* had no answer to this problem. On the contrary, by not allowing the rules of the organisation and distribution of power to be changed, it actively contributes to aggravating the problem. And the solution does not lie in the judicialisation of a system for the protection of fundamental rights, in which case the intervention of the courts even contributes to deepening the rift between the parties since it essentially constitutes a service for the "cosmopolitans" and tends to entrench their position, showing that the "non-democratic constitution" is a factor in the attack on democratic liberalism. Constitutionalism prevents society from obtaining, through "democratic oxygen", the essential elements for a naturally healthy life (for social peace). The solution must be a political reform that allows national states to restore the pact of equity that is presupposed in any project of collective social organisation and that globalisation, judicialised individualism and self-regulation of markets have not been able to promote. Only in this way will it be possible to restore confidence in institutions and their representatives, which is to say (re-)legitimise political power and its representatives. For Loughlin, *populism* is, above all, a form of reaction by national majorities to the economic and cultural subjugation to which cosmopolitan elites want to subject them and for which they mobilise the instruments of constitutionalism: supra-legal legal principles (counter-majoritarianism), individualism and the judiciary. The author identifies the "malcontents of liberalism" with the malcontents of constitutionalism, who are in fact the malcontents of globalisation—at the end of the day, they are the national middle classes, *i.e.* the majority of ordinary citizens in each country.

From yet another perspective, it seems to us that Vicki C. Jackson and Yasmin Dawood's reflection also culminates in the same result: the current problem of Western liberal democracy is based on the need for institutional reformulation. The authors start from the fact that many governments are currently unable to be responsive to their populations in meeting the needs that are fundamental to guaranteeing security and well-being, whether in terms of access to healthcare, education (and social mobility) or transport, or in guaranteeing essential freedoms such as freedom of expression and access to justice in a timely manner. And in the volume they have organised, they discuss the extent to which the realisation of these rights (what they call "effective government") must be considered an element of constitutionalism and, as such, of the realisation of liberal democracy, which is, in truth, the legitimising element of constitutionalism itself. This means that "effective government" must be guaranteed to the people as an "affirmative constitutional obligation", although the way to fulfil this obligation can be based on the deepening of self-government (which points to federalism, which since ancient times has been seen as a dimension of liberalism) and not necessarily through the courts, as is common in certain models, in which the courts take on the role of creating legal solutions to overcome institutional or functional deficiencies. Among the numerous points of reflection addressed in the book's chapters, we are particularly interested in highlighting the role that the "right to self-government" can play as a dimension of "effective government", a right that can be self-activated by public bodies on the basis of the constitutional obligation to make rights effective as a material dimension of constitutionalism and that legitimises the actions of these bodies to satisfy the well-being of the population. This is a more innovative proposal for systems such as the United States and the United Kingdom, built on the idea of constitutionalism as limited government and closer to what is already happening in European regimes with a tradition of constitutionally guaranteeing social rights, where the innovative note lies above all in the possibility of producing public self-government solutions without legislative mediation, *i.e.* by direct reference to the activation of the constitution, as a way of promoting the well-being of the population. This could be a way of overcoming social inequalities and neutralising the discontents of globalisation by deepening federalism. However, in Europe, it could lead to a worsening of the problem of autonomies and regional independence, leading to a worsening of the confrontations that are at the root of some "typical populisms" in this area of the globe.

Our conclusion from reading the above proposals together is that there is an apparent unanimity among the authors in identifying the *causes of the current threat to liberal democracy* and that they all agree on the need to *re-found* the political order *by re-establishing the principles or material dimensions of liberalism*, which have proved since antiquity to be the best way to organise community life. The differences lie above all in the constructions proposed to achieve yet another liberal re-foundation.

This means that authoritarian and hybrid constitutionalism, as well as illiberal models, will essentially tend to be, in the West, transitional paths towards *new liberal democratic constitutionalism* and will tend to disappear once the current problems have been overcome.

Political history teaches us that concepts such as *minimal democracy*, *semi-democracy* and *formal democracy* have been used in various periods to mark out regimes that can be described as hybrids because they simultaneously display characteristics of authoritarian regimes and free democratic regimes, which arise above all at times of political transition, whether from authoritarian to democratic regimes or in reverse transitions.[9] It is important to highlight two points in this regard: the first is that it is difficult to classify this type of regime as transitional since the

[9] Morlino (2022), pp. 142ff.

criterion should not be the duration of the regime but rather the purpose to be achieved, i.e. what historically characterised these regimes as transitional was above all the fact that they were not presented as a model political regime but rather as a possible nomenclature for a given concrete reality; the second point is that the concepts used have been very varied without this difference seeming to correspond to real differences in fact.

One of today's problems, however, lies in the concrete threats to liberal democracy that can be identified in regimes that can be ategorised as "mature liberal democracies" in the context of what András Sajó describes as illiberal "ruling by cheating".[10] In fact, the first remark of this phenomenon is the current prevalence of *leadership* over *ideology* has determined the centrality of the cult of certain politicians over the cult of political and ideological orientations. Voters are mobilised by the charisma of the political leader and not by the political action programme he or she presents, at a time when charisma is also not the result of the subject's special qualifications but only the result of the relevant professional actions of *party propaganda machines*, whose purpose is not even to guarantee the perpetuation of political-ideological lines but only to maintain the power of certain groups of people. From this perspective, we can say that many democracies today are "materially orientated by illiberal objects".

Secondly, staying in power is mostly achieved by weaving "webs of dependencies" and loyalties rather than by achieving good government results. Moreover, none of the public powers escapes this scenic dimension of the exercise of power, in which parliaments are transformed into mere theatres for the performance of political party representatives, who substantially change little or nothing in relation to the main public policies, and in which the courts themselves mobilise the rules of interpretation to base decisions that are less and less predictable in the light of the classic frameworks of the dimensions of the principle of the democratic rule of law. To a certain extent, each judge is a person with "prejudices" (with their own worldviews), and the more we build a model subordinated to "freedom of normative interpretation", the more we risk surprising decisions. Even in countries where the courts (and especially the constitutional courts) are not designed to meddle in political action and their members are not appointed for life, it is necessary to be critical and vigilant and to keep the discussion about the "control model" alive.

Thirdly, this verification of symptoms of the "illiberal disease" in classical democracies makes some traditional instruments of power control unproductive; for example, party self-controls, essential in the balance of parliamentary-based regimes, cease to be operative when the group (the members of the political party) is driven by an interest in perpetuating itself in power and not by ideological interest.[11]

---

[10] Sajó (2021).

[11] To a certain extent, the breaking of the "constitutional practice" that the winner of the elections is the one who governs, even if they have to do so with a parliamentary minority, which was initiated in Portugal in 2015 and then "imitated" in Spain in 2020, is also a hallmark of "illiberalism" in democratic regimes. With the rational and unbeatable foundation that the viability of a govern-

Fourthly, we return to Sajó's arguments of the governance of scams to identify another sign of illiberalism in "our" democracies: the trasvestisation of the principle of the rule of law. By this, the author means the mobilisation of principles such as the guarantee of due process for purposes that run counter to the realisation of justice. This is what happens when we witness judicial criminal investigation cases—which are usually long, complex and highly publicised in the media—which end for reasons of the defendants' guarantees, such as the statute of limitations or the inadmissibility of certain means of proof. The issue is based not on the imperfections of a justice system due to the prevalence of core values but rather on the fact that these imperfections are actively exploited in order to weaken the system. In fact, this principle of "abusive use of the guarantees of the rule of law" has taken on expansionist dimensions in various areas, such as tax law with regard to issues of aggressive tax planning and social rights with the solutions of "health tourism" and "benefit tourism", which not only weaken the more generous welfare states financially but also energise social movements of intolerance and social confrontation.

2.3 The "Constitution of the Common Good"

Having presented the diagnosis of the current crisis of democratic liberalism, it is now important to look at some proposals for re-founding the model.

Among the essays that are beginning to emerge with re-foundational proposals, the *constitutionalism of the common good* proposed by Vermeule[12] deserves our special attention. For the author, the common good corresponds to a "correctly ordered political community", which, in its own way, ends up being identified with dimensions of the Church's social doctrine. For us, the common good does not correspond to an axiological referent that can be identified with any theoretical current, only the refutation that it can correspond to the utilitarian vision of the sum of individual utilities, since we also share the idea that the law of liberal democracies needs a transcendental and ordering referent, be it the ethics of classical transcendence or the Kantian categorical imperative designed for multifaceted liberal communities,[13] and cannot be reduced to a mere self-determination of happiness. Life in society is and must be an ordered life, committed to values and duties, in which human beings will also find the well-being inherent in security, peace, order and abundance (material well-being).

ment solution with majority parliamentary support respects the majority rule because it "mirrors the social will" expressed at the ballot box, these government solutions showed that this was not the case in practice, that a pact between those who lose elections in order to selfishly implement solutions that were not those voted for by the majority of the population does not respect the rule of the majority, but rather the combination of minorities and the aggression of the true majority, and is therefore responsible for governing solutions that "irritate" society and promote radicalism.

[12] Vermeule (2022).

[13] Church (2022).

We essentially agree with the author's thinking and proposal regarding the current need to refocus the individual and political institutions and to interpret the fundamental subjective right as *ius, in other words*, as a dimension of justice that guarantees each citizen their due in a properly functioning political order (which ensures the realisation of the common good) and not as a trump card against majorities dissenting, to this extent, from Dworkin's proposal. The fundamental subjective right (which only has effective expression in inter-subjective relations with an external dimension since internal self-determination in itself does not contend with social dimensions) must be a part of the common good and not something that is intentionally exercised *against* the collective consensus. Changes in the consensus must be promoted according to the principle of tolerance and integration and not as a result of permanent *normative irritations*.

In the twenty-first century, we have witnessed struggles against order and public rules, allegedly legitimised by identity and self-determination rights—gender struggles, ethnic struggles and even economic class struggles—out of a need to reintegrate the past—pardons and recovering discriminatory pasts—which threaten to de-characterise society, destroy institutions and neutralise any collective morality. And the results of these movements are less freedom, less truth, the deconstruction of collective morality (*ius natural*) and the absence of the common good.

The author's proposal, although conceived as a reflection on American constitutionalism and the problems of a political system that is very different from the one that characterises Europeans, allows us to develop some solutions that can be *transplanted into* the European reality. Two are the most relevant to the subject of our reflection. The *first* is the relationship to be established between the constitutional text and legislative activity under the concept of *determination*. In essence, the proposal consists of transposing the method of controlling *administrative discretion* (something that most constitutional courts already do by classifying *human dignity as* "intangible" or as a founding principle) to the control of the *legislator's freedom to conform* (by fixing the meaning of fundamental principles or harmonising conflicts between them), associating *human dignity with a collective referent* (solidarity and subsidiarity). The *second* contribution of Vermeule's proposal is to refocus *interpretative power* and *legal hermeneutics* as an institutional task and not just a jurisdictional one, i.e. to ensure some preponderance for inter-institutional dialogue in place of the judicial power of the last word, with the aim of neutralising arbitrary decisions, i.e. interpretative decisions to "determine the law" without *accountability*, since reasoning and "inter-institutional challenge" neutralise arbitrary power, even if it is rational.

Vermeule's thesis is also appealing on a pragmatic level because it contains a proposal for a solution to some of the impasses of the present moment because, as the author states, the issue is not so much centred, or cannot be centred, on the search for the best architecture of control and governability but on determining the meaning of regulation. In fact, part of the democratic crisis and the crisis of liberalism is precisely the result of the loss of meaning of the objective of governance as a result of the overwhelming emphasis of studies and discussions on *governance* and the *capture theory*. It was the *game theory* that captured public regulation, rendering the definition of the *public interest* meaningless. In Vermeule's proposal for constitutionalism, this is not just a *limited government*; it must also be a *power for the realisation of security, peace and abundance* (the *common good*).

With this in mind, we believe that administrative law must also present itself as *administrative law for the achievement of the common good*, which implies some transformations in relation to the line adopted recently, especially in the context of the internationalisation of this branch of law or, perhaps more correctly, in the context of its colonisation by international law.

A second source of theoretical support for this emerges from Michel Sandel's proposals within the framework of *communitarianism*,[14] not because we identify with them but because they correctly express the errors of deviant liberalism in the form of individualism. We agree with Sandel on the need for each individual to exercise their freedom within the framework of a common *acquis*, but we remain faithful to Kantian liberalism, believing that communal harmony can be achieved without the need to impose a material dimension of the common good; we believe that it is enough to impose rules on the civility of action (the limitation of individual action) in order to safeguard the diversity of worldviews of the common good. Basically, we disagree with Sandel when he argues that liberalism is not neutral; we agree with him if this statement refers to the excesses of liberalism but not if we only take into account the organising principles of the plural community conceived by classical liberalism, a tributary of the liberalism of antiquity.

In defence of an eclectic position, we believe it is possible to fulfil a dual loyalty: to individual freedom and to the rationality of the collective, ensuring that both, although inherently conflicting, do not reach the status of predatory.

2.4 The End of Global Metanarratives of "Western Values"

In practice, this re-founding of *liberalism* will translate into various concrete actions.

The first must come from the institutions of international *governance*, which must be called upon to exercise humility by recognising the inconsistencies and excesses of the alleged virtues of global metanarratives. Neither the world nor the West can be encompassed by a discursive simplification of founding values. There is too much rich history, there are extremely important contributions and reflections whose correct and contextualised apprehension is important for (collective) and individual cultural formation and the social sciences must seek the best ways of transmitting these *acquis to* successive generations so that they can act in an informed and localised manner. We must not lose sight of the central idea that a political community can only be formed on the basis of a political society and that this requires training in information, transparency and a firm basis in the principle of rationality. One of the points that contributed to the disarticulation of the liberal community and the exacerbation of individualism was the universalisation of emotive and sensory discourse, which promoted the social revolution of replacing the cultural referents of

[14] Sandel (2012).

a "collective morality" with the apparently identitarian tribalism that comforted loneliness and ensured identity in the global context of the "one man".

Equally crucial is avoiding the instrumentalisation of scientific discourse as a vehicle for social domination and regulation through *fear and insecurity*. This is, moreover, a natural consequence of putting the rational method back into scientific discussion and overcoming deconstructionist deviations. Scientific research must recover its instruments of control (peer review) and be at the service of society and the collective interest, halting its degeneration into social engineering at the service of interest groups.

And the most important dimension is pointed out by everyone and involves the institutional redesign of liberal democratic systems within the framework of their cultural context. After all, political communities and their different forms of organisation have a history made up of failures and successes, which must first be analysed. The political sustainability of democratic liberalism presupposes a (re-) rooting of the legitimisation of power and its forms of control. The re-establishment of "trust" between the parties to this "power contract" presupposes a clear definition of the rules to which the exercise of that power is subject and the way (also according to clear rules) in which it is controlled. To this must be added the qualification and training of all those who exercise power, those who draw up the rules and those who monitor them.

It is not surprising, then, that one of the topics that most of the authors who inspire this reflection of ours as a basis for the critical and pretentiously re-founding look that we promise to take at administrative law at a later date also expounds at length on the role of *meritocracy* in the reconstruction or re-founding of the liberal democratic model.

References

Church J (2022) Kant, liberalism, and the meaning of life. Oxford University Press, Oxford

Fukuyama F (2022) Liberalism and its discontents. Profile Books, London

Holmes S (2022) The antiliberal idea. In: Sajó A, Uitz R, Holmes S (eds) Routledge handbook of illiberalism. Routledge, New York, pp 3–15

Krastev I, Holmes S (2019) The light that failed. Peguin Books, London, A Reckoning

Morlino L (2022) Hybrid Regimes. In: Sajó A, Uitz R, Holmes S (eds) Routledge handbook of illiberalism. Routledge, New York, pp 142–151

Rawls J (1971) A theory of justice, original edn. Harvard University Press, Cambridge

Rawls J (1999) A theory of justice (revised). Harvard University Press, Cambridge

Sajó A (2021) Ruling by cheating. Governance in illiberal democracy. Cambridge University Press, Cambridge

Sandel M (2010) Justice: what's the right thing to do? Peguin Books, London

Sandel M (2012) What money can't buy: the moral limits of markets. Farrar Straus Giroux, New York

Tushnet M, Bugaric B (2021) Power to the people: constitutionalism in the age of populism. Oxford University Press, Oxford

Vermeule A (2022) Common good constitutionalism: recovering the classicial legal tradition. Polity, Cambridge

Chapter 3
The "Options" of Administrative Law

In this third and final chapter of the theoretical "frameworks" that underpin our monograph, we will address the issue of the "place of administrative power" and, consequently, the "role of administrative law" in the context of the current expansionist tendencies of illiberalism and the need to re-found the founding principles or ideas of classical liberalism.

Once again, this reflection is the fruit of readings that address the same concerns, albeit from different legal and political systems and conceived from other research questions. We are referring to the support we have received from three essential works—*Law's Abnegation* by Adrian Vermeule (2016), *Law and Leviathan* by Cass R. Sunstein and Adrian Vermeule (2020) and, once again, *Constitutionalism and a Right to Effective Government?* edited by Vicki C. Jackson and Yasmin Dawood (2022)—and the way in which we articulate the questions raised there and the solutions put forward with other texts, thus seeking theoretical dialogical support for the proposals and postulates that we will present later.

In fact, we will see that the current controversial issues are the same—the real and effective power of the executive-administrative in the context of a specific institutional design (separation and control of power) and of a Western society that, for this purpose, is standardised by the same threats (to liberal society itself and to the principles on which trust is founded)—but that in the United States, it is wrapped up in the discussion about the role of the judiciary in controlling the autonomy of *agencies* and their decisions and that in continental European systems, it is rooted in the scope and autonomy of the control of the material constitutionality of public policies, as well as in the delimitation and way of recognising the areas of valuation specific to administrative activity (*discretion*).

S. Tavares da Silva, *Administrative Law for the 21st Century*,
https://doi.org/10.1007/978-3-031-55795-8_3

3.1 The Administrative Law of "Abnegation of the Law"

The differences over the "place" and "scope" of "administrative power" in American and Anglo-Saxon doctrine are clearly visible in the theses of Philip Hamburger and Adrian Vermeuler.

In 2014, Philip Hamburger published *Is Administrative Law Unlawful?*, arguing that all administrative *law* (in the sense of rules produced by administrative bodies with the aim of binding private entities, i.e. external administrative rules) is *unlawful* because it does not respect constitutional principles such as the *indelegability* of normative (legislative) powers by the representative legislative body—in the US case: Congress. The essential foundations of Hamburger's thesis are based on the *originalist constitutional interpretation* and its violation by the growing number of *agencies* with powers to dictate rules in various economic and social sectors (powers reserved for the legislative function) and powers to enforce them individually and coercively (as is typical of the administrative and judicial function), without these bodies having the necessary *democratic accountability*, since their members are not elected, and without their actions also being subject to *judicial scrutiny*, given the effects of the *Chevron doctrine* and the growing *deference* that the courts apply to the decisions of administrative authorities whenever they are not *unreasonable* or *unreasonable in relation to the meaning of the law*. For Hamburger, the *executive power of the agencies* corresponds to a type of *prerogative power*, a *power inherent to the special qualifications of those who exercise it and founded on that authority*, which constitutionalism wanted to remove with the triumph of the institutional design of parliamentarianism in the British model and which the recognition of powers to the North American Administration has mistakenly reintroduced, "out of context" of a liberal constitutional model, such as the one enshrined in the North American Constitution.

In his review of the work,[1] Vermeule harshly criticised the assumptions behind Hamburger's thesis, considering it wrong to equate the powers exercised by *agencies* with a *prerogative power* since *agencies* are always limited by the powers conferred on them by *statutes* and do not have any *prerogative* nor any (sub-)delegation of legislative power or the granting of quasi-judicial power. For Vermeule, the activity of the *agencies is characterised by the exercise of modern administrative power* (a mark of the Administration and the "bureaucracies" of the twentieth century), characterised by the power to implement/apply/execute the law, which involves the task of interpreting the law and the exercise of an activity that, in itself, constitutes an area of evaluation and decision proper to the executive power (*discretion*), without prejudice to the fact that both the interpretation of the law and *discretion* are permeable to judicial control through "intelligible principles". One of the examples that Vermeule works with is the application of tax law, recognising that the legislator (in this case the Congress) defines the tax, but it is inevitable that in the details, in the interpretation of the law, it ends up being the executive power (the tax agency)

[1] Vermeule (2015).

that concretely defines relevant aspects of the establishment of the tax base, which can then be scrutinised by the judiciary.

It is in this sequence that Vermeule ends up developing his critique of Hamburger's work—and, above all, of the echoes it is having in the Supreme Court's jurisprudence and which may be the basis of the very recent decision to revisit the *Chevron* jurisprudence[2]—and, in contrast, presents the arguments of his thesis on the "abnegation of the law", essentially arguing that the expansion of the executive power of the *agencies* is a product of the "resignation of action" on the part of legislation rather than a distortion of the American constitutional model or design.

In *Law's Abnegation*, Vermeule considers that we are dealing not with the application of a methodological principle of control of the administrative activity of *agencies* when the courts invoke the *Chevron* doctrine, or when they apply control parameters such as *arbitrary and capricious review*, but rather with a type of "sociological reaction", of "abnegation of jurists" and "courts" in the face of technical discourse, more adjusted to the "time of administrative decision-making in the modern state", which results in the abnegation of the law and the consequent legal control of them. Vermeule criticises Dworkin's thesis of the "empire of law" based on the superhuman capacity of the Hercules judge to define the law based on the interpretation of the norm, the circumstances of the case and the principles of reasonableness, coherence, and completeness of the law and its intrinsic morality. For Vermeule, the normative openings in statutes that give *agencies* the power to interpret and act, together with the jurisprudential principle of deference in control and the limitation of judicial control of their decisions to aspects of external legality, embody the legal coherence of the modern administrative state with the idiosyncratic imperatives of this new model of political organisation. The author considers it a mistake to work with the concept of separation of powers, ignoring the "administrative power" or the "power of the administrative state" and seeing it as a mere executor or implementer of the legislative power's choices, and he also considers that there are no grounds or principles that support the supremacy of the (non-elective) judicial power over the administrative power on the basis of technical arguments since both have, in theory, equal access to the law and both can have equal

[2] Remember that the Chevron doctrine (or *precedent*) was established by the 1984 Supreme Court decision (*Chevron U.S.A. v. Natural Resources Defence Council*) in which, confronted with the "legality" of a decision by the Environmental Protection Agency (EPA) regarding the interpretation of the provisions of the Clean Air Act, *the* court considered that "*if Congress has left an agency with a policy choice, the agency should get to make it, not the courts*" and instituted the "double test", according to which, if it is shown that there is a *vagueness in the rule of the statute*, the court must accept the *agency's* interpretation of its powers to act (since it is an entity subject to the *accountability of* the President), provided that this interpretation is not unreasonable with the meaning of the law, and not replace it with an interpretation set by the courts.

The *Supreme Court* announced in May 2023 that it would re-examine this *precedent* (the *Chevron* doctrine), which served as the basis for the *agencies*' power to act and which is widely criticised by Philip Hamburger in his thesis when he received the case of *Loper Bright Enterprises v. Raimondo on* "appeal". *Raimondo* discussed the legality of the decision by the *National Marine Fisheries Service (NMFS)* to make fishing companies bear the costs of having an inspector on board their vessels to monitor compliance with the rules on preventing *overfishing*.

independence from political power. In *Law's Abnegation*, the author ends up extolling the virtues (and the not ignorable reality) of administrative power and the need to scrutinise it according to the principles of the democratic rule of law.

The subject is taken up again by Vermeule in a book co-authored with Cass Sunstein in 2020,[3] in which they both present arguments for legitimising the power inherent in the modern administrative state based on the actions of the *agencies*, which many authors have been questioning, be it the defenders of *constitutional originalism* and the *non-delegation doctrine*, such as Hamburger, or the *democrats* who question the actions of the *agencies*, or even the neoliberals. The authors react against these doctrinal proposals—which they call the "New Coke"[4]—and argue that the legitimisation of regulatory power is not based solely on the popular will emanating from the democratic principle, but rather they believe that there is a material foundation legitimising legal solutions—the law's internal morality—which is achieved through procedural principles, some enshrined in or derived from the rules laid down in the *Administrative Procedure Act* (APA),[5] principles that limit that power by preconditioning the way it is exercised, either when they require a cost-benefit analysis inherent in the principle of well-being (Sunstein) or when they translate into the promotion of social welfare as the founding principle of government action (Vermeule).[6] For the authors, these material-procedural principles are sufficient to ensure respect for the rule of law in the exercise of administrative power and, as such, to guarantee the legitimacy of its actions through the "adequate control of Leviathan".

---

[3] Susntein and Vermeule (2020).

[4] The name "Coke" is inspired by the position of the English jurist Edward Coke, who at the beginning of the seventeenth century, as a parliamentarian, actively collaborated in drawing up documents to limit the absolute power of monarchs, and is considered one of the theorisers of British constitutionalism.

[5] Most of the authors refer to the principles defined by Lon Fuller in his 1969 work (The Morality of Law) as the so-called preconditions of a legal system that respects "legal morality", i.e. only rules that are produced in compliance with these parameters can be considered legitimate legal rules and, as such, binding. The principles are: *i) the* making of rules bearing in mind that this is a parameter for deciding individual cases (to make rules in the first place, ensuring that all issues are decided on a case-by-case basis); *ii)* transparency, in the sense that all those affected by the rules must be aware of them and their obligations (transparency, in the sense that affected parties are not made aware of the rules with which they must comply); *iii)* prohibition of retroactivity, in the sense that people cannot rely on current rules, and are under threat of change; *iv)* obligation to make rules understandable; *v)* prohibition of incoherence, i.e. approving rules that contradict other rules (issuance of rules that contradict each other); *vi)* prohibition of approving rules that impose obligations on people that they cannot fulfil (rules that require people to do things that they lack the power to do); *vii) the* obligation of stability, prohibiting permanent changes in rules that prevent people from directing their actions (frequent changes in rules, so that people cannot direct their action in accordance with them); *viii) the* prohibition of contradictions, in the sense of mismatches between published and announced rules and the interpretation that is then given to them in practice (a mismatch between rules as announced and rules as administered)—Susntein and Vermeule (2020), p. 40.

[6] Susntein and Vermeule (2020), p. 5.

The authors' moderate proposal, with the apparent intention of "maintaining" a moderate position of the Supreme Court in promoting the functional autonomy of administrative power, has been criticised, but it has also been praised as an important contribution to the construction of eclectic and moderate positions to face the challenges of the transition to a stronger model of control of administrative power.

One of the eclectic proposals is by Richard Epstein,[7] for whom administrative power should not be granted the breadth of freedom of action or space for free evaluation that the Chevron doctrine presupposes when it admits *deference* regarding the interpretation of the statutory powers of the *agencies*—a matter that the author describes as de *novo* normative interpretation—but neither should that space be completely neutralised, giving way to complete judicial scrutiny that covers the control of the "choices" of those entities in matters of *policy*; in these matters, according to Epstein, *deference* should be maintained. But Epstein's position has also been criticised for being based on assumptions that are theoretically balanced but difficult to realise in practice, especially in a system where legal construction is particularly shaped by judicial activity.

What is important to retain from this current methodological discussion on the foundations of the *Administrative State* and *Administrative Law* in the USA—and which essentially coincides with the reflection that must also be made in the context of *civil law* systems—are two fundamental postulates: the first is that the aforementioned *abuses of liberalism*, which have led to a worsening of citizens' living conditions and a reduction in their well-being, especially visible with the 2008 financial crisis, have led to a de-legitimisation of the regulatory state, which calls into question the need to rethink the separation of powers and the constitutional design of systems throughout the West; the second is that the responses tend to be radical, either because of the apparent weakness of the response of moderate solutions (because they lead to results that are not immediate and therefore do not excite and because they do not fully satisfy the new radical ideologies) or because of the incapacity or inability of the leadership at the centre.

3.2 Neoclassical Administrative Law

In *civil law* countries, with special emphasis on the European Union bloc, the legal discussion on the need to "reform administrative law" does not seem to have reached this dimension or sense of the problem. Perhaps this is due to the strong hegemony of the *German model* in the economy of systems, whose theoretical foundations lie in *i)* the normative force of the Constitution and the legal values enshrined therein, with special emphasis on the intangibility of the dignity of the human person, and *ii)* the effectiveness and ultimate guarantee of these values through the system of material judicial control, at the top of which we find the constitutional control of the

[7] Epstein (2020).

"powerful" *Bundesverfassungsgericht* in "dialogue" with the Court of Justice of the European Union and the European Court of Human Rights.

We could say that in the *European civil law model*, the main cultivators of *administrative law* do not seem to be concerned about the need for a new discussion on the legitimisation of the Administration's discretionary power in the context of its "extension" to "regulatory discretion" or the "discretionary action of regulatory authorities" or even the scope and control of their activity. At the European level, the discussion is neutralised from the outset by the preponderance of a *sublime* argument of the *triumph of neoclassical administrative law*, i.e. the triumph of constitutionalism and its founding values and principles and the permeability of almost all administrative activity to judicial scrutiny under the aegis of these principles, which ultimately culminates in a scrutiny of the constitutionality of the very rules that discipline administrative activity. It is the further development of this model that is at the basis of the German proposal for the so-called *new administrative law* that we mentioned in Chap. 1.

It is a solution in which the administration's space for free judgement—known as *discretion* or *discretionary power*—is part of the thesis that triumphed with the emergence of constitutionalism and the legal-normative and institutional design of the post-war era, a model in which administrative action is recognised as a space of free evaluation, in which technical decisions are excluded from judicial scrutiny, but in which the courts have the final word in defining that space of free evaluation, as well as in identifying what can be qualified as issues of a technical nature. The fact is, however, that even decisions taken in the area of free judgement are subordinate to the law, which means that they can be judicially scrutinised in the light of legal principles, some of which have a very wide methodological and semantic scope, such as the principle of equality or proportionality.

European administrative law also contributes to the apparent hegemony of the model for various reasons. It helps elevate to a supranational level, imperative for the member states, a set of founding principles of the European legal order and to limit the role of the member states in interpreting the meaning of these principle-norms through the actions of the CJEU, which both "guides" the decisions of the national courts and judges the cases in which the Commission condemns the member states for non-compliance.

If we want to characterise the current *civil law* administrative model briefly and impressively, we would say that it is, in theory, a power entirely subordinated to the law and judicially scrutinised, and as such, we would not be able to raise the kind of questions that are the basis of recent doctrinal disagreements in the United States.

But this is a reading of reality based on the theoretical design of the model that does not take into account the shortcomings and perversions that have also led to the crisis of classical liberalism and the institutions on which it is based.

Firstly, it is important to emphasise that the broad power that this model has progressively given to the courts by entrusting them with the supervision of administrative activity and normative acts in the case of constitutionality control has not been accompanied by a *reform of* this system, either in terms of the legitimacy and qualifications of the decision-makers or in terms of the guarantees of its proper functioning. In practice, this has resulted in a *permanent crisis in European justice systems*, caused by delays in decisions and the complexity of procedural management, which have become autonomous issues, discrediting the functionality of this pillar of the democratic rule of law.

Added to this is the challenge, or at least the growing theoretical doubts, about the effective democratic legitimacy underlying decisions by constitutional courts that take on an activist slant or, in less intense formulas, energise rights or principles that should limit the current way of life, as in the case of the *Bundesverfassungsgericht's* decision on climate law.

The *democratic deficit of the model of judicialisation of administrative activity* is not an entirely unrelated issue in European countries.

In a reflection based on elements of comparative public law—North American, English, French and German—Susan Rose-Ackerman argues that the Executive-Administrative State that "creates" public policies through regulation is today an unavoidable element in the democratic systems of Western constitutionalism, and it is impossible to imagine that the parliamentary legislature can fully fulfil the function of primary or innovative normative creation. In the author's view, the public administrations headed by the governments embody a *necessary* judicial technocracy, and so the reflection on the deficiencies and problems caused by the democratic deficit that this legal creation may have, must be resolved, taking for granted that this reality exists, and not based on the idea—mistaken, according to the author's thesis—that the principle of democratic legality will return to the exclusive scope of parliament. Thus, in the context of proposing solutions for the re-understanding of reality and the validation of the new model of government in the light of the democratic principle, the author proposes the recognition of a right to public policies from an executive-administrative source, whose rules are guided by a judgement of cost-benefit analysis, without being exhausted by this, but rather corresponding to a global evaluative judgement of public policies, which is a hybrid judgement, in other words, simultaneously technical and legal. The author also proposes an increase in the participation of stakeholders in the procedures for drawing up administrative rules, together with other ways of increasing the democratic legitimacy and *accountability of* primary law from an administrative source. It is important to emphasise that, in essence, the author's thesis highlights the importance of stakeholder participation as an element in legitimising these rules, but she sees this participation as a universal participation of stakeholders, in which, alongside the players in the sector (generally companies and economic groups that are investors) and the interests expressed by representatives of conflicting interests, such as consumers, trade unions and other representatives of non-technocratic civil society, must be taken into account, and this is the right way to update the current legal-political model. As we will see in the section on regulations in the new administrative law, we doubt the goodness and practicality of this proposal. Presenting itself—admittedly or implicitly—as a response to the shortcomings of a technocratic normative model, this increase in participation aims above all, in the author's words, to make the public interest effective as the realisation of the common good, in the sense of promoting collective aspirations. This is, in our opinion, one of the "cardinal sins" of the current Western governance model, which is at the root of growing populism: it replaces traditional political legitimisation with a more direct representative legitimisation, but it also replaces reason with "feelings", and from this perspective, in our view, it has proved to be a way of "throwing the baby out with the bathwater" as it increases discontent, frustration and society's resilience to economic adversity while also contributing to an increase in confrontation between groups in society and to Manichaeism. At the end of the day, it also contributes to de-legitimising constitutional models for organising power and political accountability and, thus, to the crisis of classical liberalism.

Susan Rose-Ackerman's proposal has one virtue that we would like to highlight: it is an alternative response to the growing judicialisation of administrative *law* that has characterised *civil law* models, partly also driven by *European law* and the role that the CJEU plays in its effectiveness.

It is not only the primary production of norms by the executive and administrative bodies that constitutes a challenge and a perversion of the constitutional design, but also the intervention of administrative courts can constitute and has contributed to this result in European *civil law* countries. The complexity that all the authors identify with the need to produce rules in technical and very varied areas whose legitimacy is questioned often ends up culminating in disputes that pit group interests against economic interests and are thus brought before the courts, which are asked to identify, in the specific case, the interest that should prevail and the one that should be sacrificed, which, in practice, consists of defining the public interest. In other words, the courts are asked, on the pretext of a concrete dispute, to decide a conflict between conflicting general interests, which translates into the judicialisation of the determination of the public interest. This is what happens when the court is asked to rule that a certain scientific research activity promoted by a company is illegal because it doesn't properly safeguard health protection, or when an industrial licence, which is essential for economic development, is challenged on the grounds that the activity to be carried out jeopardises environmental protection.

And the same perversion occurs when, also on the pretext of a specific dispute, the court is faced with the need to make typical public management considerations, such as the allocation of human, technical or financial resources to certain economic activities. These disputes have become recurrent in cases where the state's responsibility for omission or breach of the duty of care is questioned[8].

It is wrong to think that the courts can exercise this type of control in a routine and thorough manner. Even when these are administrative courts, i.e. courts specialising in this branch of law. The problem, contrary to what some doctrines argue, is not one of equipping the courts with more resources and more knowledge, because what is at stake in judicial control is always and only the judicial function, as it is configured in the context of the separation of powers and its independence. Scrutinising the public interest pursued by administrative power is not and cannot

[8] These are cases of state liability for omission of the duty of care, i.e. for not having the means to monitor, for not having the means to prevent or combat risks and dangers, for not having the means to diagnose, treat, etc.

be a task for the judiciary. A judicial decision based on legal principles, whether in its delimitation, interpretation or weighing up in the context of a conflict with other principles, is transformed into a judgement that, in essence, is also a primary legal production, in other words, the definition of the public interest, not least because the normative-binding nature (when there is an express system of precedents) or just the procedural-uniformising nature (when there is no system of precedents) of the judicial decision means that even if it is dictated for a case, its novelty aspires to be functionally equivalent to a rule. This is the basis of the CJEU's activity as an instrument for implementing European law.

And without much questioning of *the legitimacy of the judiciary* to produce this type of decision, initiatives to expand the production of this type of judicial decision are multiplying, with normative solutions such as *popular action* at the national level and an increase in the number of matters in which European law "opens the door" to the admission of preliminary rulings, i.e. the establishment of a *standardised public interest at the European level* that applies to diverse socio-economic realities such as those that characterise the various member states.[9] *Europeanisation* corresponds to a *denationalisation* and *acculturation of* public law under the cloak of technocracy, which contributes to the destruction of the historical idiosyncrasies of the models of constitutional government forged under the aegis of liberalism in European countries.

3.3 The Difficulties of an Eclectic Model and the Position Adopted

The alternatives for "re-constructing" classical democratic liberalism, in institutions and, above all, in society, is no easy task, as illustrated by the various reflections contained in the works published in the last 5 years by the most renowned international jurists.

In this respect, Mark Tushnet's statement that we are between the drifts of popular constitutionalism and the supremacy of the authoritarianism of the judiciary is extremely useful and illustrative.[10] Popular constitutionalism is part of the matrix of democratic liberalism, according to which citizens are political individuals, in the sense that they are interested in actively participating in public and collective life and in defining the public interest. Furthermore, the Constitution, in its prescriptive dimensions of the attribution of power, is addressed to the representative bodies of democratic power to limit them and define their corresponding functional limits (the system of *checks and balances*), and it must be interpreted by them. The judiciary

[9] Just think, for example, of the definition of a health safety parameter by the CJEU, which can serve as a judicial parameter for determining responsibility for the duty of care, and the difficulty that such diverse health systems, with very different budgets at the national level, can have in complying with them.

[10] Tushnet (2020), p. 243.

acts as the last valve in the system, as the guarantor of those rules by the powers and guarantees that they interpret those powers in a reasonable manner and, furthermore, that they respect the space for individual self-determination that embodies citizens' fundamental rights. This is why the constitution of courts and the training of judges are technical issues and not questions of legitimacy through the representation of interests. On the contrary, in Rousseau's classic conception, the judiciary is the guarantor of the very balance of powers and the neutralisation of any abuse, including of democratic power itself if it approves legislative acts that violate the Constitution.

Now, while it is true that the *judiciary* has this dimension of guarantee, it is also true that in all models, it is necessary to weigh up this power, in terms of both how judges are appointed and the scope of their powers, especially when they are recognised as having the power to control the acts of the other branches of government. Critics believe that Tushnet ends up proposing the triumph of popular constitutionalism as an alternative to the supremacy of the judiciary and that this proposal represents a kind of populism against elitism. But our reading is that Tushnet only vehemently rejects the drifts of *judicial activism* that are gaining favour in *common law* models, influenced by the European "judicioauthoritarianism" of the CJEU and the German Constitutional Court.

Perhaps it is important to remember that one of the central points of the appealing nature of proposals for judicial supremacy lies in the *authority* of its decisions, which must be accepted by everyone (the population and political and administrative institutions); otherwise, the Western democratic model of separation of powers will be completely disrupted. But it is also true that this *authority* is fragile and that many populist movements openly question the solutions, while endogenous problems with the organisation and management of the judicial system discredit the principles of the rule of law that underpin the model's credibility. The delay in justice is something that can easily be manipulated by interested parties in the light of the procedural system of guarantees and prevents the production of useful decisions (in good time) or even the enforcement of sanctions (including criminal ones), which means that the justice system becomes a *game of strategy* for the operators, a system that can be interfered with by political power and a growing source of discredit for users and the population in general. In some countries, such as Portugal, the *justice crisis* has even become a *new business opportunity*, with the system being privatised through the widespread use of *ad hoc* arbitration to resolve disputes in administrative and tax matters, where there are no guarantees of independence, impartiality or even transparency.

The position we are defending is that of *strengthening the authority of the administrative state* by re-qualifying it. We agree with the authors who argue that the *new administrative state*, or the jurigenic production of public policies by the executive branch of government or by the administrative state, is an inevitability given the complexity of interests and areas of regulation that have become autonomous. However, we would like to point out a factor that disrupts the model, which is less mentioned in the works and which lies in the excesses of the *privatisation of public regulatory tasks*. Private individuals are essential in co-administration, but only if they are subordinate to the power of the technocratic regulatory authorities. This model needs to be complemented by a *new legal relationship* between technocratic decision-making and political decision-making and by the *empowerment of the Public Administration* in other sectors and areas of activity, including recruitment and training reform—the creation of a Public Administration made up of the most capable professionals—the establishment of a system of permanent technical and ethical evaluation and the qualification of salaries and reputation.

The central idea of our reflection is that the reconstruction of the public model of classical liberalism involves the reconstruction of a Public Administration as a strong technocratic power, with indirect democratic legitimisation, whose decisions can be derogated from transparently by a responsible political power and by judicial control centred on formal procedural aspects and *last-resort* material aspects.

In essence, we have anticipated, even in title, the criticism that many will level at this model: that it is an administrative law of the *illiberal* state, and so our endeavour in the following points is to try to dispel this postulate, showing the advantages of the proposal in different concrete areas of administrative law.

References

Epstein R (2020) The dubious morality of modern administrative law. Rowman & Littlefield, London

Jackson VC, Dawood Y (eds) (2022) Constitutionalism and a right to effective government? Cambridge University Press, Cambridge

Susntein C, Vermeule A (2020) Law and leviathan. Redeeming the administrative state. The Belknap Press of Harvard University Press, Cambridge

Tushnet M (2020) Taking back the constitution. Activist judges and the next age of American law. Yale University Press, New Haven

Vermeule A (2015) 'No' review of Philip Hamburger, 'Is administrative law unlawful?'. Tex Law Rev 93:1547

Vermeule A (2016) Law's abnegation: from law's empire to the administrative state. Harvard Univeristy Press, Cambridge

Chapter 4
The "Return" of "Authoritative" Administrative Law

It is now time to start explaining the concrete dimensions of the "idea of our administrative law of authority", in other words, the administrative law with which the administrative power of the state works in the context of the new constitutional design of the modern *Administrative State*. The Administrative State has powers of primary regulation (which is jurigenic) in matters typical of public policy management and whose validity is judged by its ability to realise the public interest as a dimension of the common good, identified with the principles of *classical liberalism* (guarantee of personal self-determination within a space marked out by the constraints of community life).

The first two things we note are their *authority* and the *special form of legitimisation* that underlies their decisions, in line with the guidelines of *classical liberalism*.

In this new context, *authority* is a product of the special way in which decisions are legitimised. We are referring to decisions that are technocratic in essence (they are based on a cost-benefit analysis and other management judgements) but that need proceduralisation with para-democratic *inputs* (respect for the *principle of participation*) and rational justification that respects the *principles of transparency* and *reasonableness*. In our opinion, what characterises administrative law from the liberal (re-)foundation is the redemption of *authority as opposed to negotiation* or *collaboration*, which has characterised the current trend in *administrative law*. Today, due to economic privatisation and the reduction of exclusive public service activity, it presents itself as an administrative state that contracts, negotiates, partners, finances and reserves authority for regulation and supervision.

Classical liberalism—as we have already said—presupposes the definition of public interest objectives that define the individual's sphere of self-determination and impose a set of *fundamental community duties*. In addition to the *duty to contribute to the financing of public interest objectives* through the fulfilment of tax obligations, the state also explicitly or implicitly imposes a set of *obligations*, *prohibitions* and *conditions* on the exercise of rights, which are not *restrictions on fundamental rights*, as has sometimes been claimed in the context of an

S. Tavares da Silva, *Administrative Law for the 21st Century*, https://doi.org/10.1007/978-3-031-55795-8_4

unsustainable individualist understanding of life, but rather mere *regulations on the exercise of those rights*, with a view to harmonising them with life in the community.

The difference between restrictive rules or acts and rules or acts regulating the exercise of rights is fundamental for a correct legal framing of the issues, also in terms of the legitimacy of issuing them.

Thus, the fundamental guarantees of a democratic state governed by the rule of law dictate that an individual restriction can only be imposed on the basis of a prior normative act issued under the terms constitutionally laid down for this purpose (as a rule, through approval by parliamentary law or inscribed in a chain of parliamentary legitimisation), and an administrative normative restriction requires, where admissible, a chain of legitimisation on a parliamentary basis.[1] In a negative sense, the restriction of fundamental rights cannot be an activity of the *Administrative State*. However, *regulating the exercise of certain rights and freedoms* is clearly one of its tasks in the context of managing the common good.

In order to guarantee the *legality* of administrative activity, it is essential to proceduralise it and subject it to *a* set of control *guarantees*. The courts are no longer the main guarantors of the rights of the administrators but rather the watchdogs of *good administration*, i.e. the correct exercise of administrative power. This is not a step backwards to the mere control of legality in which discretionary activity was inscrutable, but neither is it a question of replacing an administrative decision with a judicial decision, with or without "technical support", in the name of the alleged best interests of the individual, as we have seen in recent years. It is a matter of checking, firstly, that the decision adopted by the administrative state respects the legal limits imposed on *good administration* and then—and only then—defining the terms in which material control can and should take place.

4.1 Administrative Acts

Administrative acts are the basic legal institute of German administrative law. The idea is that *administrative law* fulfils an essential function in organising life in society, limiting the arbitrariness of public and private behaviour and ensuring the pursuit of well-being. To this end, a typical form of administrative action is the unilateral issuing of *decisions* that have specific recipients and that aim to define legal situations, whether in a favourable (*e.g.* a licence or authorisation to drive, to build, to operate an economic activity that is not free, to exercise a profession), unfavourable (*e.g.* the imposition of a penalty, a demolition order, a prohibition on exercising a right) or neutral (*e.g. the* assessment of a tax, the issuing of a certificate or a title) sense.

An administrative act is traditionally associated with an aggressive and authoritative administration and in itself associates the idea of authority with the idea of

[1] Vieira de Andrade (2019).

harm or aggression. Even in the field of the so-called service administration that emerged with the welfare state, administrative acts were still associated with a (negative) idea of authority, as opposed to material operations. A typical case is the refusal of treatment or the supply of medicine by services responsible for managing health resources, which is an administrative act, while the provision of medical services or the supply of drugs is a mere material operation.

However, *administrative acts*—and in particular their litigation—are also affected by the vices or excesses of *liberalism*, to which we referred in the previous chapters.

Firstly, the *individualism* associated with *judicialism* has led to a distortion of the core character of the *administrative function* and to uncertainty in the delimitation of the administration's own area of judgement. It is possible to find examples of judicial decisions ordering the supply of a certain drug to a certain individual or imposing on the state to order them to undergo a certain medical treatment, ruling on technocratic issues through technical support for the judicial decision and ruling on the *appropriateness* of public resources in the name of protecting individual rights and, *ultimately*, the alleged *dignity of the human person.*[2]

It confuses the problem of the *Administrative State*, which is to *control the arbitrariness and abuse of executive power* (in other words, the counter-democratic dynamisation of public policies) through the intervention of judicial power that limits the exercise of executive power to the fundamental principles of liberal democratic constitutions, with the need to *control the exercise of administrative power*, which must be limited to repressing solutions for the illegitimate application of the law in the concrete case, in other words, the deviations of a concrete decision from the normative parameter.

In practice, however, establishing the difference between these realities seems complex, largely because of the *cultural mix* in which the systems are immersed.

The *common law* models, accustomed to the jurisprudence of *hard cases* that allowed *precedents to be set* and, based on them, a decision parameter for cases—in other words, a parameter that is normative, if not by its very nature, at least by its functional vocation—became inebriated with the charms of the German methodology of the "new administrative law", the legal hermeneutics of principles and the definition of the "norm of the case", believing that the judiciary should leave its traditional principles of *deference* to focus on *fixing the meaning of the norm.*

At the same time, *civil law* models, built on the methodology of hermeneutics centred on the principle of legality, have evolved towards the *principle of legality* and the *full and effective guarantee of the fundamental rights of administrators*. In this evolution, *administrators* are no longer (it even seems that they *can* no longer

[2] Many decisions of the South American constitutionalist current of so-called judicial activism (without prejudice to the conceptual differentiations that can be made in relation to this concept) are part of this, as they believe that the realisation of fundamental rights, including their interpretation, is ultimately a task for the judiciary, with or without prior law, and therefore the administration can and should be ordered to carry out individual acts whenever this type of issue is at stake—Smith (2022).

be) citizens with a legal *status* of their own, in other words, citizens with a special legal condition deriving from a functional *status* in life in society (peers in the context of the fair distribution of resources and the enjoyment of freedoms) but merely holders of fundamental rights and even supranational human rights. These "new administrators" can take legal action against individual arbitrariness in the exercise of those rights vis-à-vis others or even diffuse interests in what they believe should be the meaning and content of public policies, such as the environment, town planning or public health, always with the sponsorship of public resources. It is as if the *status of the administered*, which is a kind of *conditionality on the rights arising from life in society (limitations due to mutual respect) and the enjoyment of scarce resources*, did not exist. It is as if society were a totally free space for the exercise of arbitrariness in personal self-development, which the state and public institutions have a duty to respect and promote. In the context of the *subjectivisation of control*, the courts were required not only to control aggressive administrative acts in the face of a libertarian understanding of fundamental subjective rights, but also to actively promote means of enjoying rights to benefits (the award of benefits) or rights with a positive content (the fulfilment of positive obligations). Alongside this evolution, judicial control—through procedural changes—has also evolved towards a model of *decisions that constitute constant jurisprudence* and that, when not correctly produced and interpreted, easily slip into interference by the judiciary in normative and administrative powers, where the court ceases to be a mere guarantor of the correct functioning of the system and becomes the creator of the parameters on which the system should be based by issuing *solutions with a general vocation based on (when not on the pretext of) the solution of concrete cases.*

Over the last few years (perhaps it is more accurate to say decades), administrative acts in the field of European *civil law* models have also been used in cases that adulterate the DNA of this figure.

This is the case of *the theories of polygonal or multipolar administrative acts,* in which it is understood that an administrative decision is not limited to identifying and defining the assumptions of the *public interest* in a concrete reality but that it also involves the resolution of a potential dispute between interested parties with competing interests (*e.g.* in tendering procedures for recruitment or public procurement) or conflicting interests (*e.g.* in town planning law). This interpretation and qualification of the administrative act "opens the door" to total or intense judicial control of the decision, because if what is at stake is the weighing up of conflicting interests, we are functionally faced with the resolution of a dispute, which means that the core of the decision is of a material judicial nature, and therefore, a court can, by mobilising the same decision-making parameters that the administrative body mobilises (*e.g.* the principle of competition or the criteria for functional recruitment) and by applying the principles of conflict resolution (proportionality, reasonableness, equality) with greater propriety and mastery, identify the correct solution and modify the administrative decision without jeopardising the functional separation of powers.

But this understanding of the model is wrong, because, it elevates the presuppositions of the legal decision to a control parameter, but neutralises the typical and ineliminable presuppositions of the *administrative decision* (be it a management criterion or a criterion of organic functional aptitude); in other words, it replaces an administrative decision with a judicial decision and thereby annuls the space and content of the administration's own evaluation. The administration is no longer able to buy what it wants and needs, and it can no longer recruit those it considers most suitable for the job. This administration is no longer "fair", it is a "de-administrativeised", "functionally violated", "unauthorised" and "uncharacterised" administration. It's an administration that has no room to administer (let alone define an administrative policy), nor to qualify itself and that becomes an amorphous bureaucratic structure for the day-to-day and precarious management of affairs, judicially tutored.

The methodological-functional deviation mentioned above also has *societal, economic and developmental costs*, when it makes all decisions precarious (there is no trust and no authority in administrative decisions), makes the management of public interests uncertain (any administrative solution that is implemented is always at the mercy of judicialisation), allows administrative activity to be blocked (excessive litigation causes justice to be delayed, and this is used strategically as an element of the private management of public interests) and has contributed to a Manichean society with a permanent conflict.

Another example of the transformation of the administrative act into its substance is that which arises from *popular impugnation actions (a sort of class actions)*, which allow for the *politicisation of administrative issues* (in the sense of transmuting an administrative decision into a questioning of the public policy option that underlies it) and their consequent *judicialisation*. It is as if *administration by the courts* or the *judicialisation of public policies* could be the appropriate way to overcome the democratic shortcomings of the constitutional political system or the financial shortcomings of the state. It is to imagine that the social and economic model is deepened in a positive sense when interest groups that do not achieve sufficient political representation to interfere in the democratic definition of public policies within the framework of democratic institutions (whether in parliament, the government or elective sub-state bodies) can, at *last call*, access the courts in order to be able to make their position prevail (considering that it exists and that it is not just a sterile expedient to "make noise" and "appear" in media society). *Popular actions* have become ways of instrumentalising activism, with high procedural management costs. In practice, the systems seem condemned to not being able to discuss revising their assumptions without immediately being labelled illiberal by reactionaries.

A third example of the distortion of the legal institute of the administrative act is the judicialisation of administrative silence or inaction in cases of *non-compliance with a legal obligation*. In essence, this is a construction that requires administrative bodies to carry out an administrative act *ex officio* (without first being asked to do so by the interested party), considering that the obligation to do so results directly from a legal rule (*e.g.* awarding a contract to the company that comes first in the tender procedure). This understanding also affects the core of the administrative function, not because it "imposes" the act itself but because it interferes with the *timing of the act*. The administrative body may want to acquire that good or service or take on the new worker at a later date, more in line with a management decision, and this forced determination of the timing of the act interferes with any management decision. It is even a counter-sense because on the one hand, the call is made for the administration to adopt private management practices and criteria—the *new public management*—favouring the adoption of solutions typical of private law, but at the same time limiting the ability of administrative bodies to adopt solutions typical of private management, such as consulting the market to assess the costs of purchasing a product or service and then deciding *whether* and *when to* purchase it (without prejudice, of course, to private individuals being obliged to maintain the validity of the tender for the typical commercial term), as well as consulting the market to check the possibility of hiring a new employee and then deciding *whether* and *when to* hire them.

Part of these distortions of the administrative act regime, which essentially neutralise the authority that was traditionally inherent to it, comes from the "subjectivisation" of the control model, combined with the *individualism* that German administrative law gave to the "idea of administrative law", within the framework of a jus-fundamental conception of the exercise of administrative activity subordinated to the principle of the *rule of law*. Schmidt-Assmann[3] characterises this principle in eight essential points: *i*) subordination of administrative activity to legislative rules, *ii*) control of administrative activity by independent courts that ensure the affectivity of access to justice and the rights of administrators, *iii*) certainty of law by the legislator and case law, *iv*) prohibition of excess, *v*) prohibition of arbitrariness and guarantee of equal treatment, *vi*) legal certainty of protection of good faith before individual decisions, *vii*) right to the reinstatement of the legal position in the event of illegal actions and *viii*) right to a fair administrative procedure. This German current of understanding administrative law as fully judicially scrutinisable through the sieve of fundamental rights, ensuring that administrative acts have to respect the rights (and legitimate aspirations) of individuals and be part of a rationality that is fully controllable by the law, cancels out the space for evaluation typical of the technocratic dimension of public management and creates "irritations" and entropies in the development of public policy by neutralising its effects on individual situations through judicial decisions.

Our proposal is that the *administrative act should* return to its "original bed", in the sense of being legislatively conformed as an authoritative decision on a specific case, which should only be subject to control as such, that is, as an expression of the concretisation and application of an administrative measure whose correct application must be scrutinised and not as a pretext for scrutinising the rationality of the normative parameter that gave rise to that specific decision. This control is a *normative policy control* that must be shifted to that level and to forms of control that are appropriate and adapted to that parameter, instead of transmuting everything into a control of pseudo-restrictions of fundamental rights. This is not to say that administrative acts can become arbitrary administrative decisions; on the contrary, the duty to give reasons for the specific decision in relation to the context and the parameters

[3] Schmidt-Assmann (1993), p. 68.

that guide administrative activity is essential, as is the duty to provide the recipient with a correct understanding of the *methodological itinerary* that led to the adoption of the act. We would stress once again that the proceduralisation of administrative action is essential for the legitimacy of decisions, their transparency and the guarantee of judicial review.

4.2 The Administrative Rules

In terms of *administrative rules*, the issues have been more complex. It is important to start by emphasising that the *normative power of* the *Administrative State* is today a multifaceted reality and one of the most variable in terms of the specific constitutional designs that exist.

For the US and *common law* models, the fundamental issue has been—as we have already said—the regulatory powers of the *agencies*, which are not limited to market regulators in the form of independent administrative bodies under European law but also cover sectors such as the environment, public health or plant health.

In the case of European countries, the discussion about the normative powers of the Executive Administration may not be limited to the issue of *administrative regulations* but may also cover the primary normative acts of entities with "governmental" powers, at both the federal or the regional level, and even at the national level with regard to the emergency legislative powers of governments—a much-discussed issue with regard to the implementation of measures to combat the pandemic—or even, as is the case in Portugal, the ordinary legislative power of the Government in matters not reserved to Parliament.

Regardless of the variables of the models, what is at stake here is an impressive expansion of the normative powers of the *Administrative State* that has significantly reduced the relevance of parliaments and the legislative acts they adopt in the daily lives of citizens and, consequently, the scope for democratic representation. The transmutation of parliaments into mere stage arenas for sterile political discussion and the consequent loss of the political and legal value of the *law* is perhaps the most decisive element in the crisis of democratic liberalism today and the rise and rise of populism. It is because of this irrelevance of parliaments that democratic oppositions find it difficult to assert themselves as a credible alternative to the incumbent government. They also end up proposing radical measures and putting forward unreasonable and unworkable solutions. Everything contributes to the deadlock of democratic solutions.

Structures such as the European Union contribute even more to this distortion of the representative democratic principle at the normative level by removing the power to approve rules on the organisation of economic sectors from national parliaments. These rules are now mostly approved by directives issued by an intergovernmental structure (the Council of the EU) in which the executives of the member states participate. And the issue does not change with regard to the European Parliament's legislative output (the European Regulations), who is also a fragile democratic structure, in which representation, legitimisation and the political substratum itself (the European people) are formal categories constructed by an "intergovernmental will", which determines an indirect and distant legitimisation of the citizens, who mostly abstain from voting in these elections or vote according to an internal political perspective.[4]

The *status quo* has led to the State Budget Law being given decisive political weight as it is the essential political moment for the real and effective political subordination of the Executive to parliamentary democratic power. As a result, the budget law is no longer an instrument of day-to-day management and a structuring document for public policies but an instrument of political negotiation in the most mundane sense. The approval of the annual state budget is now a time when the Executive analyses the parliamentary composition whenever it does not have a majority in that body and seeks circumstantial compromises to ensure the continuity of the exercise of power. "European intervention" in national budgetary matters after the 2008 financial crisis only accentuated the problem of the emptying of the democratic principle and aggravated the crisis of liberal democracies.

Thus, studying administrative normative activity today is a much more complex subject than the traditional study of administrative regulations—secondary norms confined to the execution of legislative acts or the regulation of secondary aspects relating to the operation of public services.

In many countries, the issue is partially understood as a problem of constitutional law, especially when the object of study extends to the normative powers of the executive (the government) or independent regulatory bodies. But the issue must be analysed from the perspective of *public law* and the principles that must underlie the validity of setting normative parameters with innovative content, whether in terms of legitimacy, material validity or control.

In terms of *legitimisation*, there are two ways of restoring confidence in the principles of classical democratic liberalism. The first requires a *chain of democratic legitimisation*; in other words, it is obvious that Parliament no longer has the capacity to debate, approve and discuss all the issues that need to be regulated, but Parliament must have the power to legitimise the major political options and the frameworks and general principles that will then be developed and regulated by the executive and the administration. There will certainly also have to be a requalification of Parliament, within the framework of the proposals we have already mentioned for reforming the design, but without a democratic centrality, it is not possible to rebuild political freedom. The second way is to *qualify democratic participation* within the framework of the procedure for producing norms. The path has been trodden—once again—in the direction of opening up activism (*e.g.* popular initiatives), which has only contributed to noise in the system and has no useful effect. It is important that the rules are produced at the executive and regulatory level with the participation of the interested parties, those who are actually affected by the rules and who should be called upon to give a useful opinion on them at the

[4] Davies et al. (2022).

drafting and discussion stage. In short, we need a new legal regime for the sources of law (new types and new principles) that takes into account the realistic contribution that each level of decision-making can and should make.

At the level of *substantial validity*, the issue has been reduced—once again—to a judicialisation of questions, always with the aim of obtaining a judicial decision that assesses the conformity of normative solutions with the fundamental rights of those affected by those norms. In fact, the issues have been formulated—and sometimes dealt with by the competent courts (constitutional or supreme courts)—already on a level of *analytical excess*, in which the "inconvenienced" acquire the procedural status of "injured parties", regulatory measures are qualified as restrictive measures, "model changes" are treated as "illegitimate and confiscatory social setbacks" and the free conformation of the democratic legislator is neutralised by jurisprudential principiological weighting. The normative level is where the *primary democratic expression*, developed within the chain of legitimisation by reference to that *primary standard of* political choice and in accordance with the procedural rules of transparency and participation, must *prevail first and foremost.* What is more, the *inputs that concretise* the normative parameter along the production chain are, as a rule, technocratic in nature, with a view to promoting the primary public interest according to criteria of efficiency and cost-benefit analysis, which should not be disturbed or neutralised by a legal weighing up of alleged restrictions on fundamental rights or the prohibition of social setbacks, such as that called for and so often promoted by case law.

This means that our proposal regarding the control dimension presupposes, on the one hand, self-restraint on the part of the judiciary not to "accept" the transmutation of issues relating to the conception and design of primary legal-legislative options into issues of restricting fundamental rights and, on the other hand, the creation of forms of material (non-judicial) control of these political normative options, either through the institutional design of a system of *political checks and balances*, mostly based on the *power of veto*, or through the development of technocratic instruments for the "validation" of political options with no invalidating effect, such as their scrutiny by independent bodies (*e.g. fiscal councils)* that produce systematised information on the *errors* of those policy choices.

4.3 Economic Regulation and the Direction of Public Policies

A third area of activity where changes are called for in order to adjust the model to the dictates of administrative law as part of the re-founding of the liberal democratic state is that of economic regulation entrusted to independent administrative bodies responsible for directing public economic policies of a sectoral nature.

We are referring, in essence, to regulators in areas such as energy, telecommunications, transport, water and waste and, in some cases, also the environment and health. The reform should also include, albeit for other reasons, regulators in the financial sector, such as banking and financial institutions and insurance. Here, too, regulatory activity is very heterogeneous, the sectoral *leges artis* are completely different, but the objectives to be fulfilled are generally similar: to ensure that competition is maximised and the market functions correctly, which is the prerequisite for promoting well-being.

However, as we saw earlier, this regulation ensures (or can theoretically ensure) compliance with the best *standards* of technocratic regulation in the context of the idiosyncrasies of each "market", and in this activity, it mostly rests on setting authoritative (not necessarily legal) rules for the operation of these markets. In many cases, these are rules of a technical nature, with a limited number of recipients (the *players* in these markets) and which aim to guarantee the interests of end users and consumers. But the purpose of this regulation must be limited to this technical dimension, and it must not be required, as it has been, to fulfil social objectives or social regulation. Its purpose is to ensure the best functioning of the market, while the pursuit of welfare objectives and social policies is already the task of the bodies that democratically regulate public policies.

This can justify imposing (superimposed or juxtaposed) a political decision on the regulatory decision in order to guarantee concrete objectives—*e.g.* the obligation to offer goods and services at predetermined prices or with predetermined qualities. These political impositions have to be "separated" from the content of *technocratic decisions* because they are different in their *source of legitimisation*, in their *responsiveness* and *responsibility* and also in their control. Let us see.

The *imposition of public policies* (*e.g.* the requirement that all telecoms or energy supply companies have a social offer or that banking operators have service offers with certain characteristics, such as exemption from costs and fees, or service offers for certain population groups, such as young housing loans) is a measure that economic operators have to comply with and is not to be confused with the regulatory impositions that the regulator dictates to ensure the proper functioning of the market. The results of the former are the responsibility of the political power through its own instruments of democratic control, while the results of regulatory measures are the responsibility of the regulatory authority through its own control of its activity, whether through the courts or through control by independent quasi-judicial authorities. And the way in which these two types of measures are controlled is also different since the former is evaluated by the interested parties and the population in general in relation to the known elements in terms of the effectiveness of the social indicators they aim to achieve, while regulatory activity is subject to control according to the scrutiny of the technical rules on which it is based, be they general rules (efficiency, cost-benefit analysis) or those specific to each sector.

What we have seen in recent years is a situation where rules, objectives and controls are mixed, culminating in a zero-sum result for everyone. Regulatory authorities are required to devise technical rules that fulfil social functions; that is, entities that are equipped and geared towards defining technocratic rules for the functioning of markets are also required to ensure social policy objectives, removing responsibility from democratic entities—the Executive-Administration—for the effective promotion or otherwise of these social objectives, In this way, the onus for poor results in promoting public policy, whether they be regulatory in the *strict sense (e.g. market dysfunctions)* or related to the realisation of social objectives *(e.g. lack of accessible or inclusive services)*, is transferred to the regulatory bodies, which are unaccountable. In the same vein, the Government-Executive "plays" on two chessboards, claiming for itself the cases of regulatory success, even if this is essentially a technocratic measure to which it is oblivious and blaming all market failures on those entities over which it emphasises it has no power of direction or oversight.

Added to this is the fact that the European Commission—once again—intervenes in this area—along with the case law of the CJEU—in a disruptive way, either when it imposes identical measures for very different economic and sociological realities or when it condemns states for using their power of authority over economic entities to adopt relevant social measures, ending up leaving only the path of social welfare open (which is always sectarian, pernicious, incomplete and mostly ineffective). *European law is, and has been, the driving force behind neoliberalism* (the economic excess of liberalism) and the destruction of European social equity under an alleged legitimacy based on the implementation of the European social model. The limitations imposed by the European institutions (the Commission and CJEU) act, in this way, as a pretext (and most of the time as a reason) for the Executive's inability to act politically, making it possible to hold external entities responsible for failing to fulfil social welfare objectives and thus short-circuiting the chain of political-democratic accountability.

Once again, citizens—and sometimes economic operators themselves—construct fictionalised disputes, sometimes over the omission of a duty to regulate, sometimes over the omission of a duty to protect (legal or even fundamental) rights, seeking to achieve by judicial means what materially and functionally should (and can) only be ensured by political-administrative means.

In recent years, we have seen the growth of atypical regulatory phenomena as a way of reacting to the inadequacies and inconsistencies in the relationship between economic regulation and the stimulation or implementation of public policies and their socio-economic objectives. Based on the typical tools of the information society and the knowledge gained from the development of the social sciences, especially behavioural economics, *regulation* initiatives *by informal means* multiplied, taking on different names—*guidance*, *behavioural regulation*—until the publication of the work by Thaler and Sunstein,[5] which definitively "coined" this "form of regulation": *nudges*.

Today, especially after the pandemic, we are fully aware of the risks and dangers associated with this form of behavioural regulation. Its informality is also a determining factor in its arbitrariness (due to its inability to be controlled) and the dangers it entails as it energises regulation based on emotions rather than rationality, which many believe has been exploited through forms of social regulation based on fear.

In this respect, the administrative law of the re-founded liberal state is the administrative law of formal regulation, which imposes a clear *ring fence* between

[5] Thaler and Sunstein (2008).

technocratic regulation and political-social regulation and which has established appropriate forms of control, both for technocratic decisions and for the *accountability of* political-economic-social decisions.

4.4 Administrative Sanctions

Intrinsically linked to the issue of economic regulation is the question of *administrative sanctioning law* and the countless "violations" of its essence that we have seen in recent times, which we will try to summarise here.

Administrative law in civil law systems included the possibility of *sanctions* being imposed by administrative bodies for breaches of *administrative rules*—something that in *common law* systems was reserved for the judiciary. But the traditional theoretical discussion in European *civil law* countries about the *legal nature* of this *sanctioning law* as administrative law or criminal law is also well known. The proposal to consider that there is an administrative sanction law is nothing new and has been cultivated since the work of the Italian Zanobini (1924) on administrative sanctions, through to the various currents that studied the subject in the middle of the last century with the aim of promoting the *decriminalisation* of this sanction law (for violations of police and road traffic rules) because it was considered that these were unethical offences.

With different nomenclatures in the various legal systems—administrative sanctions or administrative offences—the existence of an area of *administrative law* linked to the application of sanctions is now taken for granted, including in *common law* countries,[6] especially in the field of economic regulation where one of the "powers" most feared by economic operators is precisely the power to apply financial sanctions that the regulatory authorities have under legal and statutory terms.

However, this area, too, which is typical of the exercise of a strong power of public authority, has been the subject of "intervention" by European bodies, in this case on the initiative of the ECtHR's case law, which, in line with its previous case law,[7] categorises all punitive measures (as opposed to preventive sanctions) as measures subject to the rules of criminal law. In the 2014 decision *Grande Stevens v. Italy*, the ECtHR considered that even though there are specificities in administrative regulatory sanctions that depend on the type of offence in question, there is still a "duty to bring administrative sanctioning procedures into line with the rules on the protection of human rights" since these sanctions constitute real penalties and, as such, must be subject to the principles of criminal law, such as a fair and equitable trial or *ne bis in idem*. This case law has also been elevated to a normative parameter

[6] See the UK's approval of the Regulatory Enforcement and Sanctions Act 2008.

[7] We refer to the case law of 5100/71, Engel y otros v. Países Bajos (1976) concerning military and prison disciplinary sanctions, the case of Dewer v. Belgium (1980), appeal no. 6903/75, concerning an order to close a butcher's shop for violation of price rules and case no. 8544/79, Öztürk v. Germania (1984) concerning a road traffic offence and guarantees in the sanctioning procedure.

of EU law insofar as the CJEU has considered that it should also be considered valid in the field of sanctions imposed by European bodies for infringements of *European law.*

The question does not end with whether we are dealing with administrative or criminal activity—since most European legal systems have a general legal regime to regulate the sanctioning procedure and the challenging of sanctions—or whether the competence to deal with challenges to these decisions belongs to the administrative jurisdiction or the criminal jurisdiction in systems where this differentiation exists (as is the case in Portugal and Germany). The fundamental problem lies in determining the principles that regulate this matter, especially with regard to the *measure of the sanction*, since the aim of a regulatory sanction on economic agents is to get them to change their behaviour and not engage in it, which involves a cost-benefit judgement and not a proportionality and weighting judgement, such as that presupposed in the imposition of a fine.

In fact, the ECtHR's case law on this matter seems to be one of the typical excesses of the liberal model we have come to, since it makes no sense to classify as a "human right" (a "right of man and of the citizen") the right to defence against the application of a sanction by a company that manipulates the market and inflates prices by illegitimately taking financial resources from the population or by a company that adulterates a product or service with a direct or indirect danger to the health of the citizen. It is as if the guarantees of the legitimate application of an unfavourable measure necessarily had to follow the sieve of a restriction on a fundamental right to the extent of protection against the exercise of arbitrary power. Administrative law is characterised by the practice of many acts with unfavourable content for the recipients, but their legal protection within the framework of the rule of law (the guarantee of protection against the arbitrary exercise of administrative power) is sufficiently guaranteed by the rules and principles of fair administrative procedure.

Nor does it make sense the claim that the sanctions imposed by the regulatory authorities amount to disproportionate sums that justify subjecting them to the sieve of criminal law because proportionality is a relative measure and not an absolute one, so the amounts determined in these sanctions have to be interpreted according to these parameters.

The result of this understanding of administrative sanctions law as a "special branch of criminal law" is yet another basis for *weakening the authority of administrative law*, as if it were not sufficiently capable, in terms of instruments and principles, to regulate fairly matters that affect the legal position of administrators who fail to comply with administrative rules. Furthermore, as has been emphasised in numerous studies, the control of these decisions by the courts of "criminal jurisdiction" often ends up distorting the effectiveness of the sanctions and, consequently, impeding the success of the regulatory activity.

But the tendency to *weaken the authority of administrative law* is not limited to the control of sanctioning regulatory activity and extends to other areas such as *disciplinary sanctions*, in which the violation of ethical duties and the respective punishment is no longer a question in which there are also inherent dimensions of opportunity in the exercise of that punitive power but is understood to mean that there are interested parties in the correct exercise of that power. The idea that there are third parties interested in the correct exercise of the disciplinary power neutralises any margin of discretion regarding certain dimensions of *opportunity* in the exercise of this functional power as it transmutes a wrongdoing with functional roots (a wrongdoing that affects the functioning of the administrative service) into a "normal" legal wrongdoing (a wrongdoing in which only the violation of legal rules and principles is judged). In this case, it is not just a question of weakening the authority of administrative law; it is also a question of "de-administrativising" the functional discipline of the Public Administration, in other words, de-authorising the Public Administration's internal command and control structures.

Our proposal in this section consists firstly of re-establishing the elements of administrative authority in relation to disciplinary sanctions. This internal authority is not to be confused with endogamous power or with incentives for the arbitrary exercise of power since the channels for the public denunciation of wrongdoing must be maintained, as well as public information on the results of investigations and disciplinary proceedings; the change we are calling for is that control over the aspects of the appropriateness of the exercise of that power should be maintained, such as the legal conformity of reasoned decisions on whether or not the assumptions for the specific exercise of disciplinary power have been verified, as well as the judgement on the appropriateness and proportionality of the penalty. This does not mean that these decisions are completely unreviewable by the judiciary, but rather it implies a more limited control in material terms, i.e. a control that must conform to the rationally reasoned decisions on the issues listed above.

And the same type of control limitation must exist in the context of the judicial review of large regulatory financial penalties, and the judiciary must accept the reasonableness of such measures when they are based on cost-benefit analysis judgements.

Finally, it is important to emphasise that in terms of administrative sanctions, we are witnessing a tension between two movements in opposite directions. On the one hand, computerisation, digitalisation and the massive and repetitive nature of administrative sanctioning procedures in the traditional areas of administrative police law (such as penalties for violating traffic rules, bans and disqualifications for serious or repeated non-compliance with administrative rules on food safety or for non-compliance with environmental or urban planning rules), coupled with the fact that we are in a field of legal offences devoid of ethical and social content, point to this being a suitable area to launch pilot automation solutions with AI in dispute resolution.

On the other hand, the ECtHR, intoxicated by the currents of individualism (as an excess of liberalism), seems to want to find an ethical sanctioning charge in all dissuasive behavioural regulation, as is indirectly clear from the decision in which it analyses and discusses the measure of "loss of points on driving licences".[8]

[8] See the cases of Malige v. France of 23 September 1998 and Nilsson v. Sweden of 13 December 2005.

We believe that the good solution lies in the computerisation and automation of decisions, which is the only way to prevent offenders from using the delay in justice that the resolution of these disputes (disproportionately) presupposes according to the ECtHR's requirements as a guarantee instrument for repeated non-compliance with the requirements that ensure the pursuit of the "common good".

4.5 The Administrative Legal Relationship

The last point in this perfunctory and topical analysis of some aspects of unilateral or authoritative administrative activity is a reflection on the scope and meaning of the legal-administrative relationship.

The legal-administrative relationship is characterised—as the name presupposes—by the fact that it concerns a matter (a measure adopted officially or in response to a claim made) that is (or should be) regulated by administrative law due to the legal nature of the activity carried out or the claim made. And whenever we are dealing with this type of legal relationship, we must respect the procedural rules that govern administrative activity. In essence, we can say that administrative bodies have a *legal obligation* to *respond to* the requests made by the interested parties and a duty to fulfil them insofar as this derives from the law, as well as to carry out all the acts required by law. At this point, there seem to be no doubts, uncertainties or controversial issues. A legal relationship governed by administrative law presupposes that the parties are aware of and abide by the legal rules that govern that legal relationship, precisely because it is not, in essence, an equal relationship, insofar as the administrative body is recognised as having a prerogative of authority, to be exercised under legally determined terms, either when it responds positively or negatively to the requests of the interested parties or when it performs on its own motion the acts that the law requires it to perform.

Some legal systems adopt the concept of a *legal-administrative relationship* as a criterion for determining the existence of a justiciable issue, in other words, for the functional delimitation of the courts' activity with regard to resolving disputes in administrative matters. This is a normal consequence of the subjectivist conception of litigation because if the courts are no longer focused on controlling the legality of administrative activity, but on protecting the rights and interests of those affected by that activity, it is understandable that their action is only admissible when those rights or interests are directly or indirectly affected. In principle, a court cannot be called upon by an individual to take cognisance of an unlawful administrative act *tout court* (this is the reserve of legitimacy of the competent public bodies), unless there are express rules that allow for an extension of individual legitimacy. However, the extension of the legitimacy of individuals to challenge administrative decisions cannot be unfounded or based on sterile and populist reasons.

In the same way that the court ceased to be an internal control and inspection body for the administration, it is also no longer limited to analysing the legality of administrative action.

The problem, once again, arises from the *excesses of the model.* It is as if the creators of the model do not want to accept the limits that it (like any model) presupposes and are adding legal constructions that tend to encompass, in the same conceptual model, increasingly different realities that de-characterise the model itself. Let us take a look at some of these distortions.

One of the first distortions we find in some systems is that the concept of a legal-administrative relationship still covers what is essentially a legal-political relationship. We are referring to cases of proxy protection of general goods or interests such as the environment, public health, town planning, cultural heritage and quality of life. Some legal systems—in our opinion the most rational—give independent public bodies (with the status of a non-judicial magistracy) the power to take these issues to court, also acting as mediating bodies, i.e. as bodies that receive complaints from the public, that can issue warnings to administrative bodies that are committing offences against those legal assets and that, autonomously, assess the need to take legal action to defend those legal assets, either by way of a challenge or by way of a condemnatory action (to perform legal acts or adopt behaviour). Other systems opt for *popular actions (a sort of class actions)*, i.e. extending legal standing to anyone interested in representing the defence of the allegedly damaged or threatened legal asset. In this case, the administrative legal relationship is fictionalised since there is no real subjective substrate in these proceedings because the issue brought before the court is not a legal relationship between the plaintiff and the defendant administrative body but a general and abstract interest, which the court is called upon to analyse and value in "competition" with the valuation exercise carried out by the administrative body. In our opinion, the issue takes on particularly disruptive dimensions, insofar as the control structure is presented in subjective terms, i.e. as the defence of diffuse interests (with no concrete or identifiable owner), when in essence we are merely judicialising a materially administrative activity; that is, under the guise of a false and non-existent legal relationship, we are asking the court to determine the appropriateness of administrative decisions, usually concerning major public projects or public policy guidelines.[9]

Another example of fictionalised legal relationships that we have already mentioned is that of *unlawful omissions of the duty to act*, which has to be very limited to real express impositions to act. In essence, the legal relationship that has not been established due to an unlawful omission by the administrative body must result

[9] Perhaps these excesses are beginning to be realised by the judiciary, as can be seen from the CJEU's decision in proc. T-330/18 (C-565/19P) in which a claim brought by a group of individuals against the European Parliament and the Commission seeking recognition of the inadequacy of the 2030 climate package (Directive (EU) 2018/410 Regulation (EU) 2018/842 and Regulation (EU) 2018/841) in the face of international commitments under the Paris Agreement was ruled inadmissible (for lack of standing since they had not proved their individual injury).

Along the same lines, the judgement of the Spanish Supreme Court of 24.07.2023 (3556/2023) dismissed the appeal brought by "Greenpeace España", "Ecologistas en Acción-CODA", "Oxfam Intermón", "Coordinadora de ONGS para el desarrollo" and some individuals against the Agreement of the Council of Ministers, adopted on 16.03.2021, which approved the National Integrated Energy and Climate Plan 2021-2030, considering it to be in line with the legal order.

expressly from the law or another instrument that binds its behaviour and restricts the opportunity of the duty to act. Otherwise, we would be allowing the courts, once again, to invade the administrative authority's own area of judgement in terms of defining both when to act and the available resources to be allocated to this activity.

A third example stems from the tendency to *increase the scope of anticipatory relief*, i.e. to demand that the court, in a legal relationship that does not yet legally fulfil the preconditions for being established but that is expected to be established with harmful effects for one of the parties, can be called upon to prevent that harmful effect from occurring. Here again, while in very specific cases it is possible to understand the goodness of the solution, in others, in the majority of cases, this early intervention by the court, which prevents the effectiveness of the administrative action, proves to be particularly pernicious, not only because the court always works with hypothetical judgements and, in most cases, perfunctory ones, but also because, by preventing the administrative action from taking effect and producing effects, it is yet another way of undermining the authority of the administrative power. One of the cases in which this type of decision should be banned is when the threat of injury relates to legal assets and not to individual rights or interests because, once again, what is at stake here is a primary, political dimension and not an administrative one.

It is in these excesses of *liberalism*, which have been reconverted to an alleged need to extend the protection of the rights of individuals, that we also find the universe of *alleged legal relationships that underlie the verification of unlawful administrative behaviour for breach of duty of care*. This is a legal construction based on the institute of civil liability, i.e. the legal relationships that arise as a result of non-compliance, with a certain type of fault (usually gross negligence), with legal duties to guarantee the normal functioning of public services or goods. In fact, if the state provides the population with a service (*e.g.* health or water supply), it is legally obliged to do so in accordance with normal operating rules (observing technical quality parameters) and is liable for the damage resulting from its abnormal operation.

The first issue—which, rather than being a perversion, is a difficult one—lies in making a clear distinction between what is *abnormal functioning* attributable to poor organisation or bad technical decisions (management or otherwise) and what is *functioning below the previous standard or below certain quality standards* that are attributable to underfunding due to a shortage of financial resources. This second case cannot be a source of civil liability. The fact is that these services organised by the state are community services, i.e. they are services financed by the community of those who make up the state, and their *normal quality* corresponds to the resources allocated to them by democratic decision (in budgetary choices). Thus, damage or injury attributable to a lack of financial resources is a source not of legal liability but of political liability and therefore constitutes a limit to judicial intervention. The duty of care of the guarantor state has a legal dimension and a political dimension, and only the former is regulated by the administrative law of civil liability, so only the former can be judicialised.

The second question concerns *identifying the universe of damage that can be attributed to the operation of public services*. This is the same as saying that it is necessary to understand whether all public services can be attributed or recognised as having a vocation to provide individualised services, the omission or deficient provision of which makes it possible to support a tort and the imputation of damage. We are referring, for example, to the general civil protection services, whose mission is to adopt preventive measures to reduce damage in future emergency or disaster situations. When such situations occur (*e.g.* fires, heavy rain, extreme heat waves, etc.), the civil protection service provides help to the population. This is a service that, by its nature, responds to diffuse interests and works with hypothetical scenarios according to the best available techniques, but it has been legally analysed as if it were a real public personal assistance or individual insurance service, as if there were a service whose purpose was to guarantee the non-production of harmful results from natural disasters or to repair the property damage caused by these events. The misunderstanding of the scope and function of the civil protection service and its legal structure, combined with the media's emphasis on emotions and the cultivation of the *individualistic* dimension, has led to a growing judicialisation of alleged cases of *illegitimate omission of the duty of care*, in which civil liability is imputed to the state based on the malfunctioning of these services for failing to prevent the individual production of harmful results.

This *status quo* of the *state's financial over-responsibility* and *lack of self-responsibility* has also been helped, at European level, by the *financial support tools for disaster situations.* In effect, public budgets are mobilised to insure risks that the victims could and should have mutualised through the market, i.e. by taking out insurance contracts. This public financial intervention also has the pernicious effect of treating situations that are factually different in the same way (it compensates property damage for those who have an insurance contract and those who don't) and thereby discourages responsible behaviour on the part of citizens.

This often-electioneering attitude on the part of the state distorts the perception that we are dealing with a relationship of citizenship, in which the financial support, if it exists, is first and foremost a measure of a political assistance nature (even if it later has a legal dimension in its implementation). Such public financial support is perceived by beneficiaries and potential future beneficiaries as a legal relationship *tout cour* based on a state obligation, which in reality does not exist. This is a clear symptom of the *aggressive individualism* in which society finds itself by not accepting that it has a duty to mutualise risks within the community, which means that it has the burden of contributing to their management and not just the right to be compensated in the event of injury.

But the *misuse of the legal relationship* to define the scope of the judicialisation of administrative law has also been expressed in other areas, such as the extension of the alleged *external dimensions of administrative inter-subjective relations*. In this case, there has been a "fundamentalisation" of public subjective legal positions with the aim of judicialising, under the title of an administrative issue, what is in reality a federative constitutional issue—of the correct exercise of and respect for the constitutional and legislative rules of constitutional development in terms of the vertical distribution of powers between the Federation, the State, the Administrative

Regions and the Local Authorities—or allowing the resolution of inter-organic or intra-organic conflicts under the alleged need to excuse responsibility.

A final example of this topic is the *"administrativisation" of extra-legal but economically relevant areas* in which the state intervenes with a "moralising" purpose that has a legalising effect. This is what happens in sports or gambling, when administrative bodies are created to supervise these areas. The supervisory intervention of the State Administration gives rise to theories about the legal basis of aspects of these activities, which result in questions about conflicts arising from legal-administrative relationships.

This last topic aims, once again, to illustrate the *excesses of* the current model, the disruptions it causes and the contribution it makes to the "distortion" of administrative law and the consequent crisis of the classical liberal rule of law. Refocusing administrative activity on its essence and re-establishing its authority are two essential points for re-founding the legal order of classical *liberalism.*

References

Davies K, van Munster M, Düsterhöft I (2022) Understanding European Union law, 8th edn. Routledge, New York

Schmidt-Assmann E (1993) Basic principles of German administrative law. J Indian Law Inst 35:65–91

Smith BC (2022) Judges and democratisation. Judicial independence in new democracies. Routledge, New York

Thaler R, Sunstein C (2008) Nudge: improving decisions about health, wealth, and happiness. Yale University Press

Vieira de Andrade JC (2019) Os Direitos Fundamentais na Constituição Portuguesa de 1976, 6th edn. Almedina, Coimbra

Chapter 5
The Role of "Concerted Administrative Law"

Alongside the aspects of the "crisis of the administrative law of authority" that we "brushed over" in the previous chapter, our purpose here is, also in a topical way, to go through some emblematic aspects of what we consider to be the development—enormous development—of an alleged *concerted administrative law* or one centred on *instruments of an equal legal relationship*, which have emerged over the last two decades and which, in our opinion, have accompanied and will continue to accompany the trends of this moment of "excesses" in the evolution of the "idea of administrative law".

These developments are, in part, a natural consequence of *privatisation*, whether *organisational*— with the massive creation of administrative entities in private form, through which an activity promoting a public interest is pursued under the rules of private law—or *functional*—through solutions for carrying out administrative tasks by delegating or contracting them out to private entities—or even *material*—through the "de-administration" of certain economic activities, which mostly translates into a schizophrenic legal solution of reduced initial control for increased sanctioning control *later on*, which then incorporates the disruptions already pointed out to administrative sanctioning law.

All these movements or trends that have led to the prevalence of concerted instruments over authoritarian ones have contributed—as we have already said—to the emergence of a *schizophrenic* and *bipolar administrative law*. It is schizophrenic because the interlocutor never knows if he is really dealing with a partner on an equal footing or with an authority that pursues a higher purpose than the entity with which the legal relationship in question is established. And it is *bipolar* because the entity with which the private legal person has a relationship can have sudden changes of interest, determined by external reasons, that are foreign to its interest and that override its expressed will. In short, administrative law suffers from pathologies that affect the essence of its rationality.

This so-called *administrative law, which purports to regulate relations of parity*, has been a source of disruption to classic administrative law, affecting not only the

S. Tavares da Silva, *Administrative Law for the 21st Century*,
https://doi.org/10.1007/978-3-031-55795-8_5

dimensions already mentioned but also some principles and assumptions of the essence of administrative law as an area of law centred on the pursuit and defence of the public interest. The most striking symptom of the disruption caused by the proliferation of legal solutions in this concerted administrative law is the way in which it has affected the understanding of the principle of legal certainty and the protection of legitimate expectations.[1]

The idea behind the proliferation of this type of legal-administrative instrument with a concerted structure is that since the free market is more efficient than the directed economy, administrative bodies should also act as market *players* and use the legal forms typical of private legal activity, not only in the traditional area of acquiring the goods and services necessary for the pursuit of their core tasks (the typical auxiliary recourse to private law) but also in what concerns the pursuit of the core tasks themselves.

It is in this context that even *traditional legal institutes*, such as the *public works concession* and the *public service concession*, acquire renewed legal regulation, with a decrease in the intensity of the administrative aspects of these legal institutes (the exorbitant powers of the owner of the work and the service lose relevance) and with a re-foundation of their legal assumptions. The traditional legal-acquisitive relationship, publicly informed, which allowed the pursuit of the public interest with recourse to private capital, is transmuted into an apparent *equal* legal relationship (*partnership*) for the joint pursuit of a task of general interest to the community. The power to *direct this contractual relationship*, which is functionalised to the interest of the public authority based on the chain of democratic legitimacy, is replaced by a power to *regulate* a lasting contractual relationship, autonomous from variations that may arise from political power, in other words, limiting the possibility of *modifying* the terms of that contractual relationship to aspects similar to those that support the modification of contracts in civil and commercial laws: a significant change in the circumstances on which the contractual interest was based, cases of force majeure or other aspects that tend to be technocratic. Changes in the political context (democratic predominance of another economic and social project) or public policies (sectoral aspects that require different public regulation) are only permitted if there is negotiation and consensus (imposing here an extreme complexity arising from the binding of administrative bodies to the principle of competition) or if they are accompanied by compensation corresponding to the loss of gain (sacrifice) thus imposed on the private contracting party. This often means that someone loses out with this form of administration, either efficiency, if we take into account all the contextual costs, or the capacity for democratic action, if we give precedence to the lasting effectiveness of these contracts. In any case, the *administrative law of guarantees* does not seem to have been conceived and adjusted for this form of administration.

[1] It is therefore not surprising that this century has already seen numerous monographic and collective studies on the subject of legitimate expectations in the field of administrative law, attempting to legally capture alleged transmutations of this cornerstone of law and the rule of law.

5.1 The Contract

In this context, the legal regime of the administrative contract is perhaps a hot area for the study of the subject, insofar as the creation and implementation of the legal framework of a capitalist economic model—which favours private economic initiative as opposed to state capitalism that directs sectors of economic activity—has catapulted this figure. As we have seen, contracts were initially restricted to a certain type of activity (public works contracts and public service concessions), but since the end of the last century, they have evolved into a typical, general and normal form of administrative activity (in competition with unilateral acts). In the past, the contract was essentially a way of obtaining private investment and risk sharing in the realisation of major public infrastructure works or even in the implementation and management of major public services to the population in sectors such as transport, the production and supply of electricity or postal services and telephone communications. The "private contractor" had a clear status as a guarantee of return on investment in the context of a closed economy, controlled by the state and in which profit margins were determinable and controllable. Today, the impression is given that this is not the case, that these are new areas of the market and competition, although the reality is different.

The harmonisation of conflicting interests was ensured precisely by the *special regime of the administrative contract*, which, recognising the differences from the civil contract regime—based on the principle of contractual freedom of the parties—adjusted that legal regime to the specificities of the circumstance that one of the parties did not act freely but in obedience to the dictates of the public interest. In this comprehensive model, the content of the contract could not override the need to ensure the effectiveness of the public interest, which led to a specific limitation on the *pacta sunt servanda* principle.

In many *civil law* systems, studying the administrative contract meant studying the so-called *prerogatives of public power* or the *prevalence of the public interest in* the field of long-term contracts between the state-administration and private individuals. This was also a context in which the "portfolio of administrative contracts" was not very extensive and in which many issues were resolved without recourse to the courts.

Particularly since the 1990s, the scenario has changed significantly and the main rule of public management has become the exceptionality of state intervention in key sectors of the economy. The dominant theory was that economic development lacked private capital and innovation, and therefore private management should be favoured. The state only had the role of formal owner of these activities and regulator, in the sense of organising the sectors of activity in a competitive environment and guaranteeing their proper functioning and compliance with certain targets in terms of the realisation of social rights.

Contract types and forms of public-private collaboration then multiplied, handing over more and more tasks traditionally seen as administrative to the private sector, from designing infrastructure projects (*e.g.* bridges, roads, local transport) to designing services exclusively for the public interest (*e.g.* organising activities in transport sectors that have come into mass use, such as air transport[2] or new communications services on different technologies).[3]

Within the framework of this new paradigm, the contract will firstly also be used as an instrument of management and administrative regulation, believing that the establishment of contractual obligations could replace the issuing of orders and directives and that the environment of collaboration was, if not more, at least equally capable of enabling the fulfilment of public interest objectives. Including at the internal level of administrative activity, where the contract could be imposed, for example, in interadministrative relations, in areas such as the definition of the public manager's competences, the delegation of competences and attributions to other administrative bodies in place of constitutional reforms of state organisation, or even the co-implementation of public policies by different levels of administration, to mention just the most emblematic examples.

With the widening of the scope and the heterogeneity of the forms and purposes that administrative contracts have taken on, many of the current inconsistencies that we see regarding this figure began to emerge.

Power to *expropriate privately owned goods and land* in order to build infrastructure in the public interest or "nationalise" (or regionalise or municipalise) services in the public interest is now exercised within a market framework, i.e. according to a procedure that favours acquisition by private law instruments over the direct use of the *potestas publica*. The latter can only be validly exercised through the contemporaneous payment of fair compensation for the expropriated property. This means that the arbitrary public power of expropriation has been succeeded by a legal and legally compliant public power of expropriation, which in many cases can bring economic gains for the "sacrificed". If before the "curves" in road and railway routes could be—real or fictitious—attributed to safeguarding certain rights, now they are attributed to certain opportunities.

Second, the power conferred on the state to unilaterally impose changes and terminate a contract early for reasons of public interest, resulting in the obligation to compensate for emergent damages and loss of profits within the scope of that contractual legal relationship, is in many cases no longer analysed in the light of the constraints and corresponding limited expectations that such a public law legal relationship entails, but it is almost entirely governed by the criteria that govern the uncertainties of a lasting contractual legal relationship in the light of the rules of private contract law. However, such an *environment of* degradation of the elements of publicising business relationships has given rise to the possibility that in some cases this management of long-lasting contracts could result in litigation aimed essentially at publicising the damage caused by poor private or privatised management or even errors in the design of the contractual bases.

As a third and final example, we highlight the use of contract law to guarantee environmental objectives (such as payments for ecosystem services) or social policy

[2] They are autonomous under a system of private provision of assistance services for baggage, aircraft and food for passengers and crew.

[3] The transition from voice to data communications.

objectives (such as contracts for social integration imposed in some legal systems on beneficiaries of social benefits).

It is as if the contract was born out of public law, but the law has neutralised all the elements of its *publicatio* that could jeopardise the market economy, and it is as if the market economy has colonised society and transmuted it into a market society, in which even values are transmuted into tradable goods.[4]

5.2 Outsourcing

Another example of administrative law being distorted is *outsourcing*. Presented as an essential organisational tool to make administrative activity more efficient, the external contracting of auxiliary services—that is what *outsourcing is all about*—has ended up becoming a vehicle for the predation of the basic capacities and skills of administrative bodies, a driving force behind the impoverishment of the labour market and the growing downgrading of public services.

It was presented as an important solution to create a market where there were no authority services, putting an end to legal public employment relationships in areas such as cleaning, surveillance, helping with administrative tasks, etc. "State employees" would only be those who carried out functions at the core of administrative activity (powers of authority) or functions inherent to public service (education, health, etc.). Activities ancillary to these would be provided by private service companies. In practice, this management option meant that the employees who carried out those functions began working for a private company that contracted with the administrative body to provide those services. In this way, although the service would now involve remuneration and the management (and profit) of the entity that organised that service for its subsequent supply, it would be at a lower cost to the administrative body because the risk of absences and sick leave was passed on to the company supplying the service as it would optimise that activity in competition with its counterparts. In practice, we do not know of any studies that show that this economic and financial gain for the public purse was real, and the whole agenda for decent work raises serious doubts as to whether the model is actually a good one.

However, it is not only in economic and financial terms that the *outsourcing* solution deserves reservations and criticism, but also in functional terms. Within the framework of public careers, these employees could aspire for promotion to differentiated careers through qualifications, whether these were provided internally or obtained externally, with the employee having guaranteed rights to obtain these

---

[4] Calabresi (2016) seems to consider that this economic analysis or economic modelling of different aspects of life is not only an inevitability of current times, but that it needs to be improved so that economists take into account different aspects of "choice theory" in order to contribute more effectively to the design of legal solutions, but this is a position that we do not follow, precisely because we subscribe to Sandel's (2012) thesis that there are many extra-market realities that should remain outside that universe.

qualifications and being able to be properly motivated by their managers. The *outsourcing* model does not include this type of incentive, and there is no certainty that labour laws will actually be applied in such a way as to guarantee these rights in the event of a desire to obtain new qualifications. In real terms, these lower-skilled workers have been placed in a more vulnerable situation.

One final note is that *outsourcing* has become more widespread and more complex. It is no longer "confined" to secondary, auxiliary and undifferentiated tasks, but is now used to acquire qualified services as an alternative to integrating new employees into administrative structures. Today, it is possible to find temporary labour companies that allow a hospital to purchase specialised medical services by the hour. And the lack of adequate regulation means that these professionals are better paid for providing services compared to the hourly rate they receive as civil servants and the opposite.

Regardless of the financial aspects and unequal treatment that underlie these solutions, as well as the poor regulation of the mediators and organisers of these services, a clear result of this change to the *status quo* is the downgrading of services that were previously based on public careers—which is paralleled and countered by the organisation of a "career system" in many private activities such as large law firms and the destruction of incentives for the permanent qualification of civil servants (in contradiction, moreover, with the Bologna higher education system, based on permanent learning throughout working life) and the consequent downgrading of the Public Administration.

It is essential to return to a system of meritocracy in public administration and the quality of public services based on the qualifications of civil servants. These, in turn, should be recruited through demanding knowledge tests, assessed over the course of their service by effective parameters of the quality of the service provided and productivity, and remunerated in line with the private sector.

Digital transition in public administration is a fundamental opportunity as it allows the computerisation and robotisation of procedures to free human decision-makers from many bureaucratic tasks, which are purely formal and of no scientific or practical interest, so that they can concentrate on the essentials, the substance of the job, for which fewer officials are needed, but the best the market can offer. A strong state is one that has an agile, qualified public administration whose authority is imposed by the right decisions it makes in good time.

5.3 The Delegation of Administrative Power

The *delegation of administrative power* to private organisations that collaborate with and assist the public authorities in carrying out activities and tasks in the public interest is another example of concerted administration that has become excessive and has contributed to undermining the authority of the state.

Public-private collaboration is not new to the administration model that took hold at the end of the twentieth century. *Concessions for public works and services* have a long tradition in many European countries as they have always been a useful and appropriate way of attracting private investment to carry out tasks in the public interest or to ensure that public services are endowed with innovation introduced under a private risk matrix. In essence, the granting state calls on private collaborators to build and operate a public good or service, which it must design, build and operate at its own risk, and within the scope of this activity it is bound by public service obligations, for which the state can pay it directly, in whole or in part, or it can ensure ways for them to be paid by the users of these goods or services.

The novelty lies in new activities that are not inherently public but essential to life in society and, therefore, almost always operated under a licence or authorisation granted through a contract. These are legal solutions whose rationale is sometimes difficult to understand since we are dealing with public regulation that ensures market characteristics (operators in adequate numbers and an orderly geographical distribution to ensure accessibility to the service) and reliability and quality of service (imposing qualification rules on operators and characteristics on facilities and the way in which the service is provided), given the fact that they can carry out acts of public power (e.g. inspection of vehicles that may not issue the document necessary for their circulation). But the same powers are exercised over other types of activities (e.g. pharmacies), which although they are not authorised to carry out acts of public authority, their activity is essential to guarantee public health (e.g. limiting the availability of opiates or antibiotics to holders of documents authorising them to do so).

The *delegation of public powers*, while a useful expedient for speeding up life in society by making use of existing synergies in private activity rather than creating new public services or creating new activities in a market environment rather than extending the perimeter of public administration, has the counterpoint that some changes have *altered the perception of formality and solemnity in public administration*. This has also been the case with the transition from traditional public services provided by public companies or personalised services of public administrations to services of general economic interest, which are now largely privatised. The *loss of solemnity* inevitably translates into an apparent relationship of proximity between the user and the service provider, who act in a market environment, thus generating a loss of the perception of community or public good. This is yet another deconstruction of *publicatio*, this time, curiously, by extending it, within the scope of its delegation, to market organisations.

5.4 The Promotion of Private Activities

Lastly, this model of collaborative, consensus-based administration has also been expanded by increasing *public subsidies* and broadening the range of *tax benefits*.

European public subsidy law is a way of "buying" public policy results from private operators (and in some cases also from member state administrations) and, through this, a way of shaping public policy. This does not mean that farmers have to produce what is subsidised by the Common Agricultural Policy (CAP); they can stay outside this subsidy scheme, but the weight it has on the market is so decisive that farmers can no longer compete with those who are subsidised. The same applies to electricity producers who are authorised by European law to receive *bonuses* depending on the technology used in their production.

The *right to tax benefits*, on the other hand, is another side of this public economic right, which counts as tax *expenditure* the tax revenue that it legally and voluntarily stops collecting under structural or cyclical public policy programmes that it wants to "stimulate", whether in the financial, housing or other sectors. As a rule, these economic areas "benefiting" from lower taxation correspond to primary and unjustified political choices, and control is limited to the need for the parliamentary approval of the respective legal regime, which is often not enough to ensure their reasonableness or even to dispel doubts as to the absence of interference in these choices. At other times, the legal wording used to condition the granting of these benefits is so complex that they fail to have the intended effect and become nothing more than a source of tax litigation, which explains why these forms of financial support for the economy are criticised so often.

In this case, the *pact* between economic operators, the state and taxpayers does not necessarily have to take the form of a contract; it can be regulatory in nature, but it must have an express and clear enabling legal basis since we are consciously and voluntarily introducing distortions and unequal treatment between some economic activities and others and between economic operators within these that act or do not act according to predetermined rules (e.g. create a certain number of net jobs or use wind technology to generate olives) or achieve or do not achieve certain pre-established objectives (e.g. plant a certain number of hectares of olive trees).

This is a financial way of enforcing compliance with a public policy, which, because it takes the form of a reverse order or instruction, seems to be able to be complied with more effectively. However, the negative externalities and contextual costs inherent in this form of administration are not taken into account, such as the perception of unfounded attribution of a premium to the performance of a normal economic activity by those who carry out equivalent but non-subsidised economic activities, the greater resistance to restoring legality in the event of non-compliance or irregularities in the performance of subsidised activities, all the contradictory jurisprudence that has given rise to the administrative and constitutional *dogma* of the principle of the protection of legitimate expectations and the prohibition of retroactivity or even the promotion of aggressive tax planning and the doctrinal and jurisprudential confusion surrounding the application of anti-abuse clauses.

References

Calabresi G (2016) The future of law economics. Essays in reform and recollection. Yale University Press, London

Sandel M (2012) What money can't buy: the moral limits of markets. Farrar Straus Giroux, New York

Chapter 6
State Responsibility

A legal concept that was slower to become part of the lexicon of administrative law was that of *civil liability of the state*, precisely because it was understood that *the public power (the King) did not make mistakes* and, to that extent, was *not capable of causing unlawful damage*. It was therefore a relatively long and evolutionary path for many legal systems to define a legal regime for cases of civil liability for acts of public power, largely driven by the constitutional recognition of the existence of *state liability* for violations of fundamental subjective rights.

We are not referring to the legal concepts of *expropriation* or *nationalisation of goods and companies*; that is, we are not dealing with the obligation of the state to pay the price of goods it acquires in a forced manner for duly substantiated reasons of public interest. Nor are we referring to situations that qualify as *civil requisition of goods*, *i.e.* the temporary use of a private asset for the pursuit of a public purpose or interest, nor to situations of payment of wages when military or civic services are imposed as a *civil requisition.* We are referring, in the first place, to cases in which, in the exercise of its activity, the public authority carries out unlawful acts and, for this reason, is obliged to compensate for the damage resulting from those unlawful acts.

The first type of civil liability we encountered falls within the scope of general civil liability for damage arising from material operations carried out within the scope of administrative activity, such as the cutting down of trees in a public garden that causes damage to private property *e.g.* parked cars) or personal property (*e.g.* a cut branch that hits and injures a citizen). These cases have undoubtedly always been grounds for compensation but not under an administrative law regime, because the only question here was whether it was the official operating the machine who would have to pay compensation in a personal capacity or whether it should be the administrative body at whose service he was working that would be responsible for compensation. And this was a problem that had long since been resolved by civil law with regard to commissioner liability.

S. Tavares da Silva, *Administrative Law for the 21st Century*,
https://doi.org/10.1007/978-3-031-55795-8_6

The specificity of an administrative law regime for state liability came from recognising that administrative activity could be illegal, that an administrative act of authority could be illegal and that this act could cause damage that went beyond the annulling effects of the act. This is the case, for example, of a civil servant who is unlawfully punished in disciplinary proceedings with a transfer penalty and who, in fulfilment of that penalty, is forced to sell his property and rent a house in the city to which he is transferred and, later, is proven to have been unlawfully punished. The mere cancellation of the act of transfer does not restore or reintegrate the damage he has suffered. And, as we have already said, constitutional law in some legal systems[1] enshrines the legal obligation to make full reparation for the damage arising from such unlawful acts.

This legal system, which has its origins in the obligation to reinstate the patrimonial situation of those who are harmed by unlawful acts of the administration, is being extended in the name of guaranteeing effective judicial protection. Let us look at some examples.

Firstly built on the regime of civil liability in tort, the mechanism for compensation through the state budget required the elements of an unlawful act, damage, an adequate causal link between the two and the agent's fault to be proven in court, the latter being presumed in cases where an unlawful act had been committed. Given the recognition that in many cases the subjective imputation of the unlawful act did not make it possible to establish a causal link with the damage, since the damage had occurred not as a result of individual behaviour but as a result of a failure in the organisation of the service, the right to compensation for these cases of *faute du service* was also considered, in addition to cases of *faute personnelle*.

Subsequently, it was understood that the state was also the owner of dangerous goods and activities and that, to that extent, it would have to be objectively liable for any damage they might cause, similar to the civil law of risk liability.

Liability for the other functions of the state was then added; that is, it was understood that it was not only the administrative function that could cause unlawful damage, but that the judicial function could also be a source of civil liability in the case of judicial decisions in which there were damages resulting from gross errors in the exercise of the function, as well as the legislative function when acts were passed that were clearly not in conformity with the constitution, international law or European law and cause special and abnormal damage. Although these legal regimes have little application in practice, they still have the symbolic value of ensuring full accountability for the exercise of public powers.

And in many countries, also under the influence of international jurisprudence, the obligation to compensate has also been added in cases where special and abnormal "damages" are imposed in order to safeguard public interests, as is the case, for

[1]And also European law in Article 41(3) of the Charter of Fundamental Rights of the European Union.

example, with the application of phytosanitary measures that require the slaughter of livestock.

All these legal regimes, with greater or lesser amplitude and with some regulatory variables, are perceptible and can be framed within the model of administrative law of the liberal state that we have been analysing. But the excesses of individualism that we have also been referring to critically have been projected into this sphere, and this legal concept, which a century ago was perceived as *legal nonsense* due to the maxim *the king can do no wrong,* has also become a source of irrationality due to the functionalised use of this institute as an instrument of an allegedly *responsive* and *responsible power*, which is often just an instrument of turbolitigiosity, symbolic entitlement and many iniquities.

Among the situations that we categorise as dubious in terms of rationality and social equity in the context of a liberal state, we highlight the regime of medical responsibility for the absence of informed consent and that of responsibility for the delay of justice.

The first—*medical liability for lack of informed consent*—is based on the assumption of self-determination with regard to medical treatment; that is, the individual must be freely and fully informed about the diagnosis, the treatment hypotheses, the effects of the treatment, the alternatives and the risks involved, and only then will they form a will and make a decision about the medical act. Now, what was born of a correct idea—that the doctor cannot be someone who has ascendancy over the other, especially when that other is in a vulnerable situation because of their illness—and aims for a correct ethical-legal result, which is to allow them to decide on their condition knowing the risks that may or may not arise from it—has become a pernicious and counterproductive instrument. With the exponential growth in convictions for the lack of informed consent, clinicians and hospital institutions, motivated by the tight rules imposed by professional insurance systems, prioritise their defence in some cases and thereby significantly increase the costs of preventive medicine; they turn the doctor-patient relationship into an adversarial one, instead of the personal relationship of empathy and trust that should govern these acts, and patients use this expediency as a way of obtaining monetary values resulting only from personal misfortune (injuries resulting from the illness) or from risks inherent in the therapeutic activity.

The second case—*liability for the delay of justice*—is equally dysfunctional. Largely driven by the case law of the ECtHR, European legal systems have been obliged to enshrine in legislation or incorporate into the scope of judicial decisions the situations of compensation for the delay of justice, which are accounted for in a quasi-objective way, according to the adequate time that the ECtHR has set for the delivery of decisions in due time, both at first instance and on appeal. Once again, what is presupposed in this legal regime is a virtuous idea (that a judicial decision rendered beyond a reasonable time is equivalent to a denial of justice), but one that ignores the problem's presupposition and its general and universal character and one where the solution must involve global reforms of the justice model—some of which we will refer to in the next chapter. The award of these compensations is symbolic in nature[2] and ignores the fact that, in itself, it contributes to yet another source of judicial litigation.

Other situations of widening the scope of the legal regime of state civil liability correspond to more profound changes in the understanding of the idea of administrative law, in line with growing individualism and the instrumentalisation of this area of law to the aforementioned activism.

An example of the excesses of individualism we mentioned earlier is the case of *compensation for breach of duty of care*. This is an extension of unlawfulness to situations in which there is no legal rule imposing specific administrative obligations, there is no dangerous administrative asset or activity at stake nor is there any special or abnormal damage but only fatalities, sometimes dramatic and in which the injured parties seek to charge the state with the obligation to pay compensation for a culpable omission of a duty to protect against damage caused by unforeseeable natural factors (*e.g.* fires, cliff collapses, volcanic eruptions) or factors that are impossible to control or neutralise (*e.g.* social revolutions, riots, strikes, the fall of a satellite) or even the choice of measures applied to manage situations of uncertainty.[3] In some cases, case law has evolved to include in this scope of compensation situations in which it is proven that there are clearly insufficient means of protection and surveillance. However, we believe that this reflection requires weighing up the weight of individual behavioural duties of care, attention, compliance with rules of urbanity and precaution, as well as the internalisation of other dimensions attributable to the *costs of freedom*, such as the conscious and collective choice to restrict the means of surveillance and monitoring of public spaces, which could allow the public authorities to act differently. In other words, society must make conscious choices between the costs and advantages of monitoring and surveillance and know that opting for freedom has costs, also in terms of self-responsibility.

A second example illustrating the key ideas we want to allude to is a critical appraisal of *civil liability* regimes *for violations of diffuse goods or interests*, such as civil liability for *damage to the environment* or *damage to nature*. The criticism lies not in the duty to make reparation for this type of damage but in the legal

---

[2] The only compensation at stake in these cases is the *damage caused by the delay*, which is fixed according to criteria of fairness, and not the pecuniary damage attributable to the delay by way of loss of chance, which is impossible to prove and quantify. There are some proposals to extend compensation to such cases, which is a source of ethical and legal problems because it allows a poorly functioning judicial system, which is a legal asset of the community along with other public services, to be functionalised to the interests of habitual litigants (usually companies and economic groups that buy legal services on a permanent basis) and channelled to them, and channelling financial resources that are not allocated to improving public services in general and that do not benefit occasional litigants (individuals who go to court infrequently, but usually in situations that are relevant to their personal lives) to the same extent.

[3] This topic has become especially popular in the context of the COVID-19 pandemic, in which some authors have explained the regulatory difficulties inherent in these phenomena of uncertainty—Sunstein (2021a, b) and others have claimed the obligation to compensate for damages arising from the measures they consider unconstitutional that were adopted to stop the spread of the virus, such as the compulsory closure of commercial establishments, confinement and the ban on movement Agamben (2020).

construction that underlies it. It is hard to understand the systematic inclusion of the legal system when we are talking about an economic operator who carries out an activity with an impact on the environment, the effects of which will have been reduced, minimised and considered in the light of the legal system of environmental impact assessment; who is subject to administrative offences whenever he violates environmental protection rules; and who may also be subject to administrative orders and instructions aimed at ensuring compliance with those terms. *Liability for environmental damage*, like the legal system of the polluter pays, seem to be legal systems that, rather than subjecting economic activities to the public interest and the weighing up of all the goods and interests at stake, allow for some weighing up to be done on an economic rather than legal level; that is, they allow nature and the environment to have a price, thereby contributing, on the one hand, to discrediting the model of the liberal market economy and, on the other hand, to making economic decisions that impose sacrifices on these goods and values that are politically unaccountable, by allowing the *subsequent washing of* authorisations and licences granted on the basis of the application of a civil liability system to repair the damage caused by the authorised or licensed activity.

References

Agamben G (2020) A che punto siamo? The epidemic as politics. Quodlibet, Macerata

Sunstein C (2021a) Averting catastrophe. Decision theory for COVID-19, climate change, and potential disasters of all kinds. New York University Press, New York

Sunstein C (2021b) Sludge. What stops us from getting things done and what do we do about it the. MIT Press, Cambridge

Chapter 7
The Control of Administrative Activity

All the dimensions of administrative law and their respective transformations that we alluded to in the previous chapters have a special relevance and impact on the *control of administrative activity*. It is important to emphasise that one of the main effects of the *excesses* attributed to *individualism* is the corresponding *excessive litigation to which it* gives rise due to the *massification* of *disputes* and the attempt to match all of them to violations of fundamental rights—a reality for which the judiciary has not prepared itself and that is at the root of the "alleged problem" of the delay in justice. Another effect, more dramatic for the disruption of the social and normative model of liberal states, is the *judicialisation of political issues* or, if we prefer, the instrumental politicisation of judicial *control*, aggravated by the *mediatisation of jurisdictional* conflicts.

These two problems, on which we will focus our analysis, inescapably contribute to exhausting the capacity of the judicial services and to hindering their normal functioning—since many of these fictional, instrumental or merely futile disputes often take on an urgent and priority nature and delay the real administrative disputes, which are essential both for the functioning of the economy and for social peace.

7.1 The Massification of Litigation and the Delay in Justice

The first of the problems we identified—the *massification of litigation*—led to the visible and most discussed side of the issue: the so-called *delay of justice*, which has since gained the status of an autonomous legal-jurisdictional issue within the jurisdiction of the ECtHR. In fact, the Council of Europe drew up a maxim based on Article 6 of the ECHR: "Delay in justice is a denial of justice"; defined parameters for the appropriate timing of legal proceedings; and built up a condemnatory case law, which many courts are obliged to follow, resulting in a quasi-objective liability

S. Tavares da Silva, *Administrative Law for the 21st Century*,
https://doi.org/10.1007/978-3-031-55795-8_7

for the *autonomous damage caused by delay in justice*.[1] This case law generates countless inequities and dysfunctionalities.

The *delay in justice*, which is a problem, would also end up partially transmuting the very nature of the judicial function: firstly, by allowing recourse to the courts to be functionalised to interests other than the resolution of the dispute;[2] secondly, by justifying and leveraging the expansion of alternative and privatised dispute resolution solutions on public matters outside state courts;[3] and thirdly, by contributing in a decisive way to the discrediting of one of the pillars of the rule of law.

The exponential growth in administrative law litigation—the kind we are dealing with in this study—is primarily associated with the growth of public regulation in a general sense. It is the *legislative increase in situations in which there is regulatory, ordering, supervisory, enabling, providing or other intervention by the Administration* that leads to the increase in litigation in matters of administrative law. Secondly, there are the other situations that we have described as potentially pathological, whether they are those in which the scope of the interests affected or targeted by legally prescribed administrative action is widened, or the scope of the rights and interests protected by legal principles is recognised, or the range of duties arising from this for administrative bodies.

In fact, we are witnessing a kind of *schizophrenia in the conception of the liberal state*, in which administrative intervention is criticised, describing it as *restrictive of rights* (*e.g.* by making it more difficult to sell and consume substances that are harmful to public health), and at the same time, the diametrically opposite effect is criticised, attributing to an allegedly passive attitude on the part of administrative bodies an illicit act due to the omission of duties of care to which concrete damage is sought. And so, a life situation can give rise to various disputes, some even based on legal solutions that are incompatible with each other.[4]

---

[1] The exceptions that can apparently justify exceeding the appropriate time limits for the definitive resolution of disputes are related to the inadequate procedural conduct of the parties (which is always disputed and difficult to prove) or to a particular complexity (which is also difficult to prove)—judgements of the ECtHR "Buchholz v. Germany" (06.05.81); "Pretto v. Austria" (08.12.83); "Obermeier v. Austria" (28.06.90); "Moreira" (23.06.87); "Lechner and Hess v. Austria" (28.06.90); "Italy" (08.12.83); "Lechner and Hess v. Austria" (23.04.87); "Obermeier v. Austria" (28.06.90); "Moreira de Azevedo v. Portugal" (28.08.91); "Pélissier and Sassi v. France" (25.03.99); "Bayrak v. Germany" (20.12.01); "Scordino v. Italy" (29.03.2006); "Riccardi Pizzati v. Italy" (29.03.2006); "Martins Castro e Alves Correia de Castro v. Portugal" (10.09.2008).

[2] Merely bringing an action can satisfy interests such as "delaying" the fulfilment of financial and credit obligations, it can be a way of "dragging" the defendant into a fictitious conflict (knowing that this fact will only be revealed after a significant amount of time), casting an anathema on him from which the plaintiff or a third party derives a benefit (e.g. compromising his political or administrative election or his business suitability).

[3] In some countries—Portugal being a relevant example in this context for the wrong reasons—the *delay in justice* is grounds for the privatisation of justice in areas where the legal conformity of the exercise of public powers is judged, as is the case with arbitration in tax and administrative matters.

[4] A businessman who is sued by his creditors in insolvency proceedings and at the same time by the tax authorities for not paying the taxes assessed against him on time may end up defending himself in the insolvency proceedings on the ground that he has no liquidity due to tax enforcement and

But the main reason for the *failure* of the judicial control of administrative activity is that phenomena such as the *massification of litigation*, *public hyper-regulation* of life and the economy and the social transformation resulting from the litigious instigation of social networks, to name just a few examples, have not been accompanied by a *reformulation* of the control of administrative activity itself. In other words, the system has been confronted with massification, complexity and changing mentalities without a responsive and re-founding solution and continues to look for an answer using traditional tools—procedural reforms, increased human resources and the use of new technologies—proving incapable of presenting truly innovative solutions able to overcoming these constraints.

There is no investment in *preventing judicialisation*. The first watchword for a healthy society should be the prevention of litigation, and the commitment to a *responsive* administration. On the contrary, the scenario is one of a set of policy guidelines for managing administrative litigation (e.g. arbitration of disputes with subsequent control by the courts or the creation of independent bodies for specific areas such as public procurement but with a merely optional nature), which, as well as proving unsuccessful, raises concerns when their promotion is insisted upon. It is as if there were an interest in presenting and promoting solutions that have been proven to be ineffective.

What is more, the idea has become widespread in some systems that *only a judicial* or *court-based decision* is capable of guaranteeing the constitutional aims of the model for controlling the legality of administrative activity, leaving solutions that are more suited to current needs in the background.

In this regard, the German doctrine is right to warn of the need to "*organise*" *the control of administrative activity according to objectives and methods*[5] because there are marked differences between annulling, sanctioning, modifying and optimising an administrative decision, and these differences must be accompanied by different and appropriate means of control. And these types of control must also be adapted to the content of the decision being scrutinised, the principle of the rule of law and the guarantee of respect for the proper areas of administrative judgement, which are essential to the proper functioning of a liberal democratic society.

may end up justifying his insolvency on the ground that he was forced to pay taxes that were not due (due to an illegal assessment), but which took years to resolve in court. Ultimately, he could even sue the state and demand compensation for the *delay in justice* and another for *responsibility for the malfunctioning of the tax services* that caused him to lose liquidity and consequently lose his economic activity. A process which, ultimately, could transfer part of the economic and financial risk inherent in their poor business performance to taxpayers.

[5] Kahl (2009), p. 431. One of the objectives is to understand decisions and reduce the "noise" from them Kahneman et al. (2021).

7.2 Internal Controls

A first example of adapting control systems to new challenges is the "revitalisation" of traditional forms of *internal control* of administrative activity and the creation of new forms of this kind. They are the only ones that can effectively control the *optimisation* of the administrative decision; that is, it is the *modification* (and not the annulment) of the decision that makes it possible to achieve the *optimisation* of its control, and this result often cannot come from annulment. This is because *modification*, which must correspond to the exercise of a still administrative power, can only be the result of internal control. The *modification of an unlawful administrative decision*, either because it is the result of an incorrect interpretation of the law or because it is the result of a decision taken with errors in the factual assumptions, makes it possible to immediately and fully satisfy the claim of the recipient harmed by that decision and dispel any expectations based on a different decision; it makes it possible, in short, to restore the law (the integrity of the normative solution if it had been violated) and social peace by clarifying the terms of the dispute. *Annulment*, when we are dealing with an act with positive content, requires the administrative body to *repeat* the decision, and this repetition may not have a single foreseeable content (even if it is not a renewable act), and this new decision may result in another legal proceedings. The optimisation of control in these cases is achieved through the intervention of a qualified and independent administrative power of control, which can expressly indicate in the decision of the dispute the administrative solution(s) to be adopted and not, as is now being proposed (and verified), by an extension of judicial power in the context of the enforcement of annulment decisions. In the latter case, we are moving towards solutions that dilute the functional differences between deciding and controlling, and the optimising solution we advocate is the one that once again highlights these differences.

Thus, one of the *widespread errors* in reforms of the control of administrative activity is to consider that *only external controls*, and preferably judicial ones, constitute a real control or, better still, a real guarantee of the interests and rights whose restoration is sought through this means of resolving disputes. Judicial control, being of a different functional kind to administrative activity, can never result in the *modification* of the administrative decision and, to that extent, should be reserved for cases in which the appropriate response is based on *annulment* and *cassation*.

Let us take a look at some examples where *internal controls* are indispensable for the correct and efficient control of administrative activity.

Firstly, there is the *control of decisions regarding the implementation of public policies*. This does not concern the *definition of the public policy to be pursued*—the objectives to be achieved in each area of state intervention—which is a *political issue*. Due to their intrinsic nature, political issues are excluded from being examined by the administrative courts and are subject to the typical forms of political control through the democratic instruments provided for in the Constitution: in addition to electoral processes for bodies with legislative powers, there are demonstrations, meetings, strikes, public expression of dissent, popular legislative initiative or even the right of resistance when the respective conditions are met. As for the *way in which* those political objectives (those primary choices) are *implemented*, by means of instruments typical of administrative activity—planning, public information and, lastly, the approval of regulations, the carrying out of administrative acts, the conclusion of administrative contracts or mere material operations—non-judicial forms of control have become widespread, especially in relation to the first stages of this procedure—namely planning and the design of strategies—with the aim of ensuring the fulfilment of objectives that are not *entirely or directly* legal according to a classic or traditional view of the law, such as *efficiency* and *sustainability*.

Despite its tendency to be excluded from judicial activity, the impact of control at this early stage of *public policy implementation* is very important, firstly, because it imposes a separation between the level of the political decision and the activity of its implementation; secondly, because it is based on a dedicated structure, both in terms of documentary support, as is the case with *strategies* in general (which are low-legal instruments, most of which have a function limited to an auxiliary hermeneutic tool), and in terms of institutional support, which is usually based on "mission units", i.e. autonomous departments of administrative bodies, almost always without being a typical form of administrative organisation, given their limited nature in time (*e.g.* without being presented as a public institute); and, thirdly, because this structure already includes elements of internal control, i.e. because these structures are equipped with elements to *monitor* the level and quality of execution and to *review* decisions in the event of complaints. Within the scope of this power of *internal control* in response to complaints or claims, a distinction must be made between cases in which the decisions are administrative acts, in which case the *review must be limited* to the rules and principles of the general law on administrative activity and those in which we are dealing with secondary choices or options, where discretion prevails and in which the challenge centres on aspects relating to expediency (fulfilment of strategic objectives) rather than legality. In the majority of cases, disputes require the court to take the place of administrative and even governmental bodies in balancing the various public interests at stake—for example, economic, environmental, cultural and social development—in order to produce a different decision. In some legal systems, this outcome is permitted and encouraged by popular actions. In others, where this procedural expedient is not provided for, there is a sophisticated scheme for subjectivising the interests in conflict (e.g. environmental interests are personalised in the protection of the fundamental rights of future generations or young generations; cultural interests in the protection of indigenous communities), which also opens the door to the judicial control of aspects of the timeliness of decisions to implement public policies.

These forms of internal control relating to the implementation of a public policy (*e.g.* decarbonisation of the electricity sector, the fight against corruption)—*monitoring, auditing and control stricto sensu*—are not subject to legal rules and principles, only to public interest objectives, and for this reason, their control is not judicial (there is no power to coercively impose compliance with targets, nor are there differentiated subjective interests in meeting these targets), but control must be ensured, with moments of publicity (public reports, barometers, dissemination of statistics), which allows interested parties to *make a critical judgement* on the actions of those entities or even a prospective judgement on the results.

The existence of these internal controls is linked to the judicial control of acts of authority (or other types of administrative activity) that may subsequently be adopted and that are harmful to the subjective positions of the administered. In the subsequent legal proceedings the legality and legal compliance of the specific measure is discussed, rather than the appropriateness of the choice of means to implement the public policy. It will be said that this proposal is inherently a reduction in the guarantee of the protection of the interests of the administered, to which we reply that it is not; what exists is an *adaptation of the form of control to the type of interests to be protected*. Where diffuse or group interests are at stake, the type of control must be abstract and based on judgements that cover the appropriateness of the measure, and to this end, the type of control is internal. Where only an illegality in the actual implementation of the measure is being discussed, the control should be judicial.

There are other areas where these *internal controls* can also be essential in reducing legal disputes, such as administrative *inspection* and *verification* activities. We are referring to the police control of public safety—through the *inspection* and *verification* of the legality of staying in the territory or compliance with safety rules for road traffic—and other forms of guaranteeing personal integrity—*health inspections* in terms of the safety of facilities or food safety—all of which are based on the use of public powers, the proceduralisation of the exercise of those powers in respect for the rights of those inspected and the application of administrative sanctions. Guaranteeing the *functioning of services* neutralises future conflicts and reduces some of the litigation between public bodies and those inspected.

A third example worth highlighting is that of *independent control bodies*, which are organically part of the administrative structure, although their activity is not subject to any kind of public power (hierarchical, superintendence or guardianship), and the law guarantees them administrative and financial autonomy for the independent exercise of their competences. This includes the bodies responsible for ensuring the uniform application of public procurement rules, those responsible for reviewing tax acts or even those responsible for resolving consumer disputes. This type of entity does not have—nor can it or should it have—administrative decision-making powers; that is, it cannot substitute itself for the powers of the controlled entities—a public entity that checks the legality of documents in a public tender—or an award act cannot substitute itself for the contracting authority and produce the tender document without the defect or carry out the award act instead. But as an administrative body, it can and must fully scrutinise discretionary decisions and can, *without substituting itself*, define the content of the administrative decision to be taken. It cannot substitute itself for the body competent to make the decision, but it can indicate the content of the decision to be made, since it is a body of the same functional type. And this is a dimension of the *efficiency and effectiveness* of this form of control, which cannot and should not be achieved by extending the power of judicial control. The unreasonableness of transferring this type of control to the judiciary means that in some European countries, "technical judges" are currently on the staff of higher courts and trained in engineering, economics or other scientific areas, who are then also entrusted with the task of "producing" decisions of a purely legal-procedural nature.

Close to the example just given is the *evaluation and control of results*, which is proliferating today in sensitive areas such as combating corruption and guaranteeing the financial integrity of the state. This is a form of control that is generally "entrusted" to independent political and constitutional entities, particularly in the financial area (court of auditors, *independent fiscal institutions*, *anti-corruption agencies*). The increase in the areas in which the state operates, with the corresponding increase in public spending, the organisational complexity of the Public Administration (direct central administration, indirect administration, the state business sector, autonomous territorial administrations, corporate and institutional autonomies) and the inherent distribution of budgetary funds and their control, together with the growing scarcity of public resources (due to the decrease in tax revenue), have led to an increased concern with *good public financial management*. Thus, a *new area of administrative law* emerged, allied to financial law, in which more than checking the legality and integrity of the acts that determine public spending, new forms of control were instituted to ensure the *efficiency of public management*. And this control—especially the control of the *efficiency of public spending*—can and has taken on a complex, inconclusive character and, in itself, has also been responsible for many inefficiencies.

In what we can call the *European legal-normative bloc*, this control of the efficiency of public spending is at the root of the legal regime for *public procurement*. Established in the 1990s, the legal framework for public procurement was presented as a way of promoting the new privatised and liberalised economic model. In order for a liberalised environment to exist, it was essential that suppliers of goods and services were able to compete fully with each other, offering their goods and services on the market and prospering in this environment through their capabilities, expressed in the acceptance of goods and services by consumers, whether through the quality of the service or product or through price.

In this context, "public administrations" were seen as consumers who influenced or could influence and distort the market, and it was therefore essential to ensure that "public procurement" was in line with the principle of competition, which led to the creation of the public procurement regime. However, this solution to a relatively simple and reasonable question, which had a more or less clear answer, turned out to be too complex. In the original version, public entities and some that acted under concession or authorisation in regulated sectors, known under European public procurement law as "contracting authorities", were legally obliged to purchase goods and services according to "market logic"; in other words, once the characteristics of the goods and services to be purchased had been defined, the lowest price bid was to be chosen after a competitive procedure, in which competitors that did not act according to market rules (because they were, for example, in breach of public tax or social security obligations) would be excluded.

However, with each new European legislative package on public procurement, the complexity has grown from the idea of complementing the objectives to be pursued with this legal regime, especially environmental (green purchasing[6]) and social (responsible purchasing), which then gave way to *strategic purchasing* (taking advantage of public procurement to regulate markets), ending up turning this legal regime into a source of dubious legality (*e.g.* each supplier of services or goods sets up multiple companies in order to be able to "circumvent" periodic legal limits on the supply of goods) and its control in a tangle of problems between control of legality/lawfulness and control of efficiency.[7]

Studies on public procurement are being carried out almost everywhere in the world, both because of the economic importance of the expenditure covered by this legal regime and because of the volume of litigation it generates.

This is not an exclusively European issue. On the contrary, the studies cover both the OECD and non-OECD worlds and their relationship with the WTO guidelines (WTO agreement on government procurement). Public procurement is an emblematic case of the increase in public and private context costs that ends up denying the fulfilment of the objectives of efficiency and competition in the name of which the legal regime was established. Perhaps this is why the new virtuous objectives of strategic public procurement are being proclaimed,[8] in order to hide the numerous systematic problems (*e.g.* the exponential increase in useful illegalities, the trivialisation of corruption and "related crimes" in public management, the predation and misrepresentation of traditional administrative dogma with "economese" concepts or concepts devoid of legal-ethical weight, which reflexively lead to the degradation of almost all procedural rules into irregularities with no annulment of decisions) that the complexification of this legal regime has brought about.

Still in the area of *internal control*, we must finally stress the important role played by *institutional administrative design*, not only in terms of administrative and political-administrative organisation when we refer to federal structures but also in terms of the internal and functional organisation of services, with the need to have new methodologies for appointing *leaders* and for interdepartmental decisions. As this is an area of public administration and not law in the strict sense, it is nonetheless important to highlight that the institutional design of public administration—the areas of activity that should have autonomy (administrative, financial and even functional), those that should be subject to permanent supervision, those that should be personalised and those that should be presented as shared services—is a

[6] The European rules and their transposition into the domestic law of the member states have, in some cases, turned out to be a jurisprudential nightmare, due to the obvious lack of legality in the densification of control parameters for concepts such as the most advantageous tender in the light of the life cycle of products, to give just one example.

[7] In addition to the permanent divergences between the interpretations determined by the case law of the CJEU and those applied by the various courts of the member states, there is also the potential contradiction between the interpretation and application of these rules in the context of the control of legality carried out by the courts and the control of efficiency that is formulated by the Court of Auditors, which can give rise to jurisprudential divergences for which there are no adequate procedural procedures to resolve them.

[8] Public procurement as a promoter of productivity, sustainable development, well-being, the digital transition and even societal change.

very important area in guaranteeing the optimisation of results, which, ultimately, is always the satisfaction of the population's needs. But in addition to this, today there is a need for efficiency, productivity, innovation and quality, something that also requires relevant dimensions in the choice of leadership. *Depoliticising* the management of services that can and should be depoliticised and ensuring the political *chain of command* that guarantees effective action is fundamental. To this end, it is also important to produce knowledge in this area, to have good public administration training schools, to ensure rigorous recruitment of civil servants and to guarantee the qualifications of managers. In many countries, this implies a different model from the one that exists today, in which administrative posts are more or less veiled extensions of the party structures in power. Controlling access to public administration means neutralising some of the litigation that results from decisions that are illegal because they are misleading.

7.3 Judicial Oversight

Improving and/or instituting the forms of internal control mentioned above optimises results and reduces litigation, but obviously not to a sufficient extent to dispense with the external judicial control of administrative activity, which also needs to be reflected on and updated.

Firstly, it is important to analyse the existing models at the world and European levels—council of state, courts of separate jurisdiction and courts of specialised competence within a common jurisdiction.

The models in which there is a "French-style" Council of State are those in which the supreme control body of the state's administrative activity is divided into two types of functions: an *advisory one*, dedicated to issuing opinions on draft laws and the respective administrative regulations, and a *judicial one*, in which it functions as the supreme court of the administrative jurisdiction, with very limited powers, merely cassatory of illegalities, what explains why this activity was entrusted to a control body that was not the common jurisdiction.[9]

The "German-style" models of separate jurisdiction, on the other hand, are based on the traditional assumption that the control of administrative activity is different from a party process because instead of being faced with an action largely conceived by the parties in the light of the dispositive principle, in administrative jurisdiction, we find a typified set of procedural means to control a certain type of administrative activity, in particular acts of authority.

These two models ended up evolving in the twentieth century towards a model of full or (quasi-full) judicial control, based on the objective of guaranteeing the full and effective protection of the legally protected rights and

---

[9] On the powers and rationale behind the creation of the Conseil d'État as a response to the increase in administrative activity and the corresponding litigation, *see* Freedeman (1961).

interests of the administrators, with a significant part of the specificity of judicial control of this activity being relegated to discussions about the functional limits arising from discretion. To this extent, we would say that, given the growing evolution of the model towards full jurisdiction litigation—based on an extension of the dispositive principle and an increasing number of legal duties imposed on the judge to collaborate with the parties to ensure the production of a decision on the substantive issue in dispute (which corresponds to a "reading" of the administrative process in accordance with the fundamental guarantee of the rights of the administered)—the autonomy of the administrative jurisdiction is today, for the most part, a choice of organisation and judicial policy, rather than a real need motivated by the specificities of the control of administrative activity.

It is perhaps for this reason that the continental control model itself, designed on the basis of the specificities of administrative litigation—centred on the review of the legality of acts of authority carried out by a public authority—has, to a certain extent, blurred its originalities and moved closer to *common law* systems, which, in turn, have also undergone an important evolution in the sense of reducing the preponderance of *deference* cases.

In order to understand the differences and the *pros and cons* of each model, it is interesting to study the experiences of Eastern European countries in the context of the transition from the authoritarian communist model to the European guidelines and how they perceive the options, doubts and solutions involved in each of the classic models. In many cases, although the continental model is the closest and the one that most easily corresponds to the traditional legal culture of those countries, everyone recognises the virtues that the *common law* model represents due to the tradition of independence of the judges, the way in which the decision corresponds to a combination of votes and not to a false impersonal and institutional consensus of a collective of magistrates and the preponderance that the case and the parties assume there, compared to a legalistic, conceptual and interpretative assessment, which is inherent in the continental model.[10]

At the European Union level, it seems that all the models are in crisis and that the *digitalisation of justice*, combined with *smart justice*, will put an end to the difference between the models since they will all converge in the study of the threats and opportunities that these tools present to combat the backwardness of justice.

In the context of this reflection, it is also worth highlighting the fact that the judicial control of administrative activity, with special emphasis on the control of acts of authority that harm subjective rights, has developed, also in contrast to constitutionality control, in other words, distinguishing itself from it.

---

[10] Interestingly, Kühn argues that the *common law* model is more resilient in guaranteeing the rule of law in the face of threats from illiberalism—Kühn (2021), p. 1239.

However, both the Europeanisation and internationalisation of the judicial protection of fundamental rights[11] and the judicial construction of the extension of the direct effects of fundamental rights[12] would end up transforming administrative courts into courts that guarantee the effectiveness of fundamental rights rather than courts that control the legality of administrative action. This triumph of rights "framed" administrative law and distorted administrative justice, stripping it of the uniqueness that presided over the models built on that concept. Today, controlling the administration means guaranteeing the rights of the administered, *even* in the face of changes in political-legislative options with democratic backing. This is not to say that some aspects of these rights should not be guaranteed but to emphasise that this development *also* represents a change in the perception of the exercise of democratic power, since it reduces, in practice, the range of options that can actually be adopted in scenarios of ideological change of government following elections. In addition, the privatised and liberalised economic model, based on the concession of public services and goods and the granting of authorisations and licences for long periods of time, combined with the much shorter electoral cycles, has contributed (as we have already explained) to discrediting the electoral process as a way of changing the course of public policies and has placed the courts as a counter-power or *gatekeeper* to these changes, which leads to the second problem we wanted to analyse: the blurring of the boundary between law and politics.

By giving the courts the role of the guardian of the rights of the administered—covering a very significant range of powers, from neutralising the effects of administrative decisions that expropriate or quasi-expropriate rights, or even those that impose some social setback, to measures that only reflexively protect subjective rights, as in the case of actions to protect diffuse interests—the system becomes an instrument for blocking the adoption and implementation of public policies by the government, if not a real instrument that requires the government to adopt policies.[13] And this means that the courts are no longer systematically located in the institutional design of the separation of powers, in a position external to political power, but become part of its game. It has become difficult to accurately distinguish

[11] There is a preponderant role in the EU area with the growing extension of the "self-attributed" powers of the CJEU through the interpretation of the ECHR, which seeks to influence and condition the political and administrative activity of the States Parties. Regardless of the position we may adopt on the merits or demerits of these decisions, we cannot ignore the fact that they are the result of undemocratic power, exclusively legitimised by a conventional system of international law, which is now being reinforced by the "adoption" of some of these *standards of* interpretation by the CJEU.

[12] We are essentially referring to the "victory" of the thesis that economic, social and cultural rights are also directly binding on the state, either when they are configured or interpreted as rights analogous to rights, freedoms and guarantees (and therefore benefit from their *self-executing* character), or when it is understood that the legal regimes that gave them effect cannot be modified by the simple triumph in the democratic game of a different political option, such measures being dependent on the limits imposed on restrictive laws.

[13] We are referring, for example, to the decision of the German Federal Court on the climate law: 1 BvR 2656/18, 1 BvR 288/20, 1 BvR 96/20, 1 BvR 78/20.

between an administrative act and a political act, as we have already said, and for this reason, it is also becoming increasingly complex to isolate a judicial decision from the political arena and, therefore, to isolate judges from the political struggle.

And everyone—citizens, political actors and judges—perceives this change and alters their behaviour. On the one hand, the political discourse is judicialised (the courts are responsible for the inefficiencies of political action); on the other hand, in many court decisions, we find public policy arguments (the court decides according to the outcome of the decision, using principles to get there and not as a result of the law laid down or predisposed by the democratic power); and finally, many judicial disputes in administrative matters arise with exclusively political purposes, sponsored by instrumental legitimacies and exclusively aimed at making newspaper headlines and feeding the *media*.

These processes contribute to discrediting the traditional mission of justice, distorting or belittling its function and, fundamentally, creating disruption in the Western model of classical liberalism.

7.4 Anti-fraud Control

A characteristic of the Western political-normative model and liberal economy, as opposed to those of authoritarian regimes, has always been the reduced weight of corruption. The liberalised and mostly unregulated environment in which economic activities took place did not allow, nor was it suitable, for webs of interests to be woven with the aim of defrauding the rules. *Corruption*, by definition, implies the practice of an act of public power in order to obtain an advantage, so the fewer the public acts that were necessary for life in society, the fewer possibilities there were to commercialise the exercise of power.

With the *regulatory state*, the terms of the equation have changed. Due to the need to carry out acts of regulatory public power, the state is now present in many areas of personal, business, social and institutional life in which it was previously absent or had a minimal presence, and this presence is necessarily a source of legal problems and also an opportunity to market the exercise of power. There is a proliferation of *criminal offences* applicable to those who exercise public functions and, in that context, carry out acts with the intention of obtaining an advantage (for undue receipt of an advantage, for active and passive corruption, for the appropriation of public money, for intentionally causing or allowing to cause damage to public affairs, for violations of secrecy), and this offence is extended to those who are related to public decision-makers. New concepts and areas emerge in the field of ethics, such as *integrity* or *probity* in the exercise of administrative activity or public service. Various *codes of conduct* have been instituted in public administrations. But the main problem with all these instruments for preventing and combating deviations in the exercise of public power (the *compliance* strategy) is the excess and lack of articulation and well-defined boundaries between them, which, added to their overlapping and contradictory cross-effects, ends up producing ineffective and counterproductive results. These pernicious effects are enhanced by the phenomena already described, such as the manipulation of information and its digital transmission through direct channels that are not filtered by credibility instruments.

But there are actually two more pernicious indirect effects that emerge from the way this type of control is currently organised: firstly, the relegation or attempted relegation to criminal offences of many situations of mere administrative illegality and, secondly, the consequent social alarm arising from the perception that there are very high levels of corruption in the public administration.

The *technicality of legal discourse* prevents citizens (and sometimes even the *media*) from fully realising the difference between the ethical and legal disvalue associated with voluntary or involuntary non-compliance with procedural rules that do not affect the substance of the decision (for example, failure to hear the interested party before the decision is made) and that associated with the violation of rules and principles that materially affect the legal conformity of the decision (for example, excluding a candidate from a civil service competition because he professes a certain religion). However, the issue is not one of a lack of legal literacy but one of real difficulty in drawing the boundaries between offences and even in correctly perceiving and weighing up the disvalues associated with behaviour that breaks the rules and the corresponding sanctions. Let us look at some examples.

Firstly, in hyper-regulated environments, it is very difficult to comply scrupulously with all the rules, which is why the re-regulation that came with the privatisation of the economy has exponentially increased the risk of illegalities, i.e. violations of the rules. The Europeanisation of public policies and the internal market has been combined with this regulation, in which many areas of the market and free private initiative have also come to rely on new and intense regulation and corresponding administrative supervision invested with sanctioning powers in matters such as food safety, consumer protection, producer responsibility, patent and copyright guarantees and competition regulation itself, to name but a few examples. Areas that in certain legal systems are part of administrative law and the respective sanctioning acts are challenged in administrative jurisdictions, while in others, they are referred to ordinary civil/penal jurisdictions. Especially in competition law and the regulation of the banking and financial sector, administrative offences (concerted practices or abuse of a dominant position) and criminal offences (such as insider dealing and market manipulation) are confused. This *status quo* means that the public's perception of the areas of finance, banking and the regulation of major public economic services is presented as a mishmash of private interests that capture the public interest and thus distort the correct understanding of the role of the regulatory state.

Secondly, in some cases, the pursuit of the public interest can jeopardise compliance with certain rules (*e.g.* a prior hearing does not take place so as not to jeopardise the urgent performance of an administrative act), which can give rise to a dispute as to whether or not there was justified urgency and whether the administration's action was in breach of the law or should be qualified as lawful despite the "deviation from the procedure rule". Close to this example are the situations that Luhmann[14] identifies, in the grey area between legality and illegality, as "useful

[14] Luhmann (1972), pp. 304–305.

illegality" (*brauchbare ilegalität*), i.e. cases in which the agent consciously commits a violation of a rule (an illegality) for the benefit of the public interest and cases in which the "justification of the illegal conduct", combined with the virtue of the result, allow the illegality to be highlighted and the disvalue of the offence to be degraded.

Thirdly, there are cases in which the ethical and legal disvalue results from the intentionality of the conduct and not from the result of the action (as happens in situations of corruption for a lawful act), which raises two types of problems: one associated with proving intentionality (not always easy) and the other concerning the maintenance or annulment of the act, which although lawful in its content was carried out for illicit reasons. And these doubts are even more pertinent when we are faced with situations of undue receipt of an advantage, i.e. where the disvalue is exhausted in the conduct of the agent, who accepts an advantage for the production of a result (for example, the practice of an administrative act), which would always be produced even though the provider of the advantage does not know it.

Fourthly, European subsidy law is responsible for the dissemination of another concept of "illegality", linked to *irregularity* and *non-compliance with obligations* due to the failure to achieve the objectives predetermined by the political programmes that support the subsidies awarded, and this compliance is assessed objectively and not subjectively; that is, unless otherwise stated, there is non-compliance whenever the result is not achieved, regardless of the conduct adopted by the beneficiary. Thus, in the field of European subsidies contracted under various public policy programmes, with particular emphasis on the common agricultural policy and regional development, the "sanction" (the result) applicable to those who defraud the system by receiving a subsidy without the intention of fulfilling the obligations assumed in return and without making any effort or activity in this direction and that which falls on those who try to fulfil the obligation but fail to achieve the result, can be identical. And this solution is dictated by the *principle of respect for the integrity of the European budget*; in other words, since the budget is intended to pay for a result, when that result is not achieved, regardless of the reason behind the failure to fulfil that objective, that money must be returned.

Fifthly, also in public procurement, many disputes raise questions of formal illegality in which the annulment of acts seems disproportionate, either because it reduces competition by excluding certain bidders or proposals or because it forces a new procedure and, to that extent, postpones the acquisition of the service or good. But on the other hand, the formalities laid down by law are the way the legislator has defined to ensure equal treatment between candidates, because they are a simple way of standardising and monitoring the certification of requirements that are considered essential in mass procedures, which means that their scrupulous compliance ultimately aims to guarantee competition objectives, equal treatment and a reduction in fraud and illicit practices. It is up to the legislator to correctly weigh up the consequences of not complying with the formalities laid down by law and to avoid making excessive or pointless demands. Still on the subject of public procurement, it is interesting to make a reference to the *self-cleaning* solutions that the legislator has enshrined as a way of overcoming impediments due to unfitness. This is an institute that, in its own way, is close to the principles underlying *restorative justice*, although, unlike *restorative justice*, in this case, the validation of *self-cleaning* by administrative bodies is sufficient, and there is no instrument for "restoring empathy" with citizens or consumer groups whose rights or interests have been harmed. Essentially, a competitor who has been convicted of violating market rules (*e.g.* for participating in a cartel) is not on an equal footing with the others and would therefore be excluded from the possibility of contracting with the contracting authority. But the European legislator allows him to adopt measures to "rehabilitate" or "reintegrate" himself and thus be admitted to the public procurement procedure and the conclusion of the future contract. The CJEU, in line with the objectives of European law to maximise efficiency in the internal market and to minimise the limits to full competition between economic operators, has adopted a very favourable interpretation of the operability of *self-cleaning* solutions. The legitimate doubts that this legal regime raises are whether we are dealing with an unavoidable instrument to ensure the proper functioning of the European internal market and whether the general benefits it brings (in terms of the economic and financial results of market prices) are proportionally sustainable in the face of the public perception that a criminal offence can be "self-cleaned" just to ensure the principles of the functioning of the market economy, in other words, whether ethics succumbs (or should succumb) to the prevalence of the market economy.

Finally, the solution adopted by European law and "exported" to the member states in the fight against corruption, based on the role of *whistleblowers*, is also worthy of mention and critical reflection. The legal regime protecting these "whistleblowers" is presented in the recitals of Directive (EU) 2019/1937 as the appropriate and most effective solution for protecting and re-establishing European Union law. The issue is complex, but our doubts can be expressed in the form of two questions: Is an inquisitorial legal system built on a model of anonymous complaints compatible with the European normative model, which was erected in reaction to the Church's inquisition with a revolution based on the enunciation of rights of freedom and which overcame the authoritarian models of the twentieth century with a constitutionalism of rights of freedom? Is it desirable, in the context of a society that sees the state as an institution for guaranteeing personal rights, to have a legal system that encourages the initiative of public authorities based on human disvalues (policing others, envy)? In fact, this instrument of control seems, to a certain extent, to be one of the examples of *civic vigilantism*[15] associated with the failure of the institutions of the democratic rule of law and the attempt by certain social groups to impose their "morality", which is why it does not deserve our sympathy.

[15] Olsen and Tuovinen (2023), pp. 1–22.

7.5 Mediation and Mediated Conflict Resolution, the Institutionalisation of the Judiciary and *Smart Justice*

One of the ways that many legal systems have adopted to solve the problem of mass access to justice and the length of court proceedings is the generalised use of *alternative forms of conflict resolution*, including in the field of public law issues, with particular emphasis on *arbitration* and *mediation*.

The resolution of disputes goes back to the genesis of jurisprudential activity, and the way in which this task was organised (especially in *civil law* models) is tributary to the origins of praetorian law, in which the authority of the decision came from its content and the corresponding authority of the person who handed it down, an authority that was a result of the prestige of the decision-makers, who were also appointed by the ruling *power* and were part of that power.[16] The need to guarantee a degree of uniformity in these decisions then began to emerge, which led to justice and law being built around two ideas: *i*) the need to codify or positivise the parameters of decisions as an instrument of equality and uniformity of criteria for resolving disputes and *ii*) the correct definition of the circumstances of the case as essential elements for finding the right solution. But the jurisprudential activity we are referring to was related to civil or criminal law disputes. There was no "jurisprudence on acts of power": they imposed themselves and were valid because they emanated from a source of power.

Alternative dispute resolution is tributary to this *jurisprudential* and *praetorian* origin of the law. Basically, there are only two determining points: the resolution of the dispute in a manner recognised as such by the parties and a fundamental emphasis on the authority of those who exercise the activity of composing the conflict, either through the application of positive law or through recourse to equity or either through a binding heteronomous decision (as is typical of arbitration) or through a decision made by the parties with the help of a third party (mediation).

In the twentieth century, *alternative dispute resolution* presented itself as the appropriate response to the need to "de-stateise" the resolution of disputes between states and between states and companies from third countries. Thus, in the context of the *enforcement* and juridification of international law (previously exclusively political) and in the context of replacing diplomacy with the juridicity of foreign investment conflicts (essential in promoting the economic model underlying globalisation), institutes such as international tribunals and quasi-judicial solutions (*e.g.* WTO dispute settlement panels) gained particular prominence, albeit with limited effectiveness of the respective condemnatory decisions, as well as international investment arbitration (especially that carried out on the basis of the so-called ICSID system).

In the twenty-first century, *alternative dispute resolution* has spread to more areas: with the *i*) generalisation of arbitration systems for consumer disputes and justices of the peace for cases of low relevance (both economically and socially), *ii*)

[16] Lushkov (2020).

legalisation and judicialisation of disputes in the area of sports, and *iii*) proliferation of the ideals of *restorative justice* and the emergence of forms of *police mediation* in areas of complex criminality, mostly due to deficits in social education. Almost all of these cases are instruments that aim to neutralise the effects of the massification of litigation through the *privatisation* or *de-judicialisation* of dispute resolution instruments. The essential question is whether these instruments can be applied in the context of resolving administrative law disputes. The response in European legal and regulatory systems has been very conservative,[17] mainly due to the numerous difficulties that arise from the need to guarantee the impartiality of arbitrators and the non-disruption of the separation of powers model, based on the independence of the judiciary. It should also be emphasised that this type of litigation is mostly based on issues that conflict with the principle of legality and, therefore, it makes no sense to resort to mechanisms for settling disputes designed to favour the predominance of fairness criteria.

It is interesting to note, however, that alternative dispute resolution instruments are sometimes promoted and defended on the ground of the special *expertise* that is needed to understand and resolve the dispute, given the technicality that underlies it. This argument is, in our opinion, a false one, if we consider what we have already said about internal controls and their appropriateness and usefulness in the context of technical and complex issues in administrative law, especially the management and implementation of public policies.

In fact, a large part of the assumptions on which judicial power is based will have to be (and already are) rethought in light of the introduction of the *digitalisation of justice* and the *smart justice* tools provided by *artificial intelligence* (AI). This is a very important moment in the transition of models, which implies an epistemological break similar to the one introduced with the creation of *judicial review*. At that time, it was a question of imposing limits on (democratic) *power* through *constitutionalisation* and the review of *the constitutionality of laws* entrusted to the Constitutional Courts. Now it is about designing and creating *robotised* solutions that dictate the legal solution to a dispute based on a combination of *database* and *machine learning* techniques. In other words, what is at stake is the ability that has been developed to create *algorithms* that are able, in terms of deciding the law, to access a giant volume of information in terms of jurisprudential precedents, legislation and parameters of legal interpretation, combined with the development of learning algorithms, which perfect the techniques of the former and which will be able to indicate the most coherent and reasonable solution for the case. Experiences that are already in practice involve tools such as *i*) virtual assistants who help judges construct coherent, rational legal reasoning based on precedent information; *ii*) automated and robotised decision-making in lower-value matters (e.g. road traffic

[17] An exception to this rule is Portugal, where there is a widespread and well-established legal system for arbitrating administrative contracts (which only doesn't deserve more criticism because it would have to come from those who carry out this very lucrative arbitration activity) and even a legal system for arbitration in tax matters.

offences, civil litigation) that can be appealed to a human judge; and *iii*) jurisprudential simulators that indicate the likely direction of a decision.

While this new world of *algorithms at the service of justice* is being discussed and countless experiments are being developed—particularly as a response to the robotisation of administrative decisions in mass procedures in areas such as immigration, taxation or even the allocation of social benefits—with a view to improving results, the neutralisation of discrimination ("natural" due to historical data that encompass moments in social evolution when there was no equal treatment) or even proving the model's effectiveness, philosophers discuss the *ethical issues* of AI and whether or not these robotic instruments can perceive ethical, cultural and even humanistic issues. Perhaps for this reason and because the European Union has already adopted a legal regime regulating AI, that is expected to *moderate the pace* of the introduction of this phenomenon, in the light of a *precautionary principle*, which is expected to have a global spreading effect, as happened with the European personal data protection regime, AI cannot be seen as the immediate solution to the problem we seek to identify and address in this brief study, and also for this reason, it does not merit further development here.

References

Freedeman CE (1961) The conseil d'état in modern France. AMS Press, New York

Kahl W (2009) Begriff, funktionen und konzepte von kontrolle. In Hoffmann-Riem, Schmidt-Assmann, Vosskuhle (eds.), Grundlagen des verwaltungsrechts, III, C. H. Beck Verlag, München, pp 427-540

Kahneman D, Sibony O, Sunstein C (2021) Noise: a flaw in human judgement. Little Brown Spark, Boston

Kühn Z (2021) The judiciary in illiberal states. German Law J 22:1231–1246

Luhmann N (1972) Funktionen und Folgen formaler Organisation, 2nd edn. Duncker & Humblot, Berlin

Lushkov A (2020) Magistracy and the historiography of the Roman Republic. Cambridge University Press, Cambridge

Olsen T, Tuovinen J (2023) Between militant democracy and citizen vigilantism: using citizens' assemblies to keep parties democratic. Glob Constitutionalism:1–22

Chapter 8
Conclusions

It is difficult to draw conclusions at the end of such an eclectic text that perhaps the only virtue we can point to—if we can point to any—is to have briefly tried to make the reader aware of two problems that we consider to be growing in the current panorama of administrative *law* in states that are part of the normative bloc of liberal states—whether they are part of the *civil law bloc* or the *common law* bloc—and that threaten the democratic rule of law on which we have built our legal systems and our common life: the first is the *excesses of individualism* present in recent legal regimes and jurisprudential movements that are leading to the legalisation of *the tyranny of minorities* and *economic deregulation,* and the second is the *alienation of ancestral community values* on which we have built our *collective ethics* based on respect and *tolerance,* which has been perverted and put to the test through campaigns of disinformation and manipulation of information, with the aim of breaking up our cultural community.

The boundaries between these two disruptive elements of our legal and ethical-cultural model are not easy to draw because the *excesses of individualism* also affect community values and economic excesses, and deregulation also contributes to social Manichaeism. And both destroy the *ethos* of democratic systems, transmuting the perception of the political system from a common good into an instrument of repression and corruption and politicians from people invested by popular choice in positions of managing the common interest and goods, according to a winning ideological proposal, into party "officials" at the service of private interests and, therefore, whose activities are questionable and must be scrupulously scrutinised.

The corollary of this work, in line with the proposal of this brief manuscript, will be organised into *concluding triads* of general administrative law concepts, with the identification of the concept present in its the genetic idea, the distorted concept to which it gave rise and the concept to be constructed in order to impose *liberal administrative law*.

S. Tavares da Silva, *Administrative Law for the 21st Century*, https://doi.org/10.1007/978-3-031-55795-8_8

First Conclusive Triad: "Public Interest—Public Policy—Political Programme"

Administrative law—as we have tried to show in this brief work—arises from the need to create and control an organisational structure for implementing and enforcing the general interest defined by a politically organised community. Political bodies are conceived according to an institutional design that guarantees the popular legitimisation of the power in which they are invested to act on behalf of those they represent and the distribution between them of various forms of action that ensure that purpose and, at the same time, mutual control between them. Once the public interest to be pursued jointly has been defined at this level, it is up to the administrative level to choose the ways of realising that public interest. And there is an *administrative public interest* that is identified with the choice of forms of action to realise the public (policy) interest, the design of instruments for financial control and good administration and the identification in *concrete terms* of how the politically defined public interest is to be realised. The original or genetic idea of the *public interest* is that of a functional dimension of administrative activity as power, both in the selection of the means of action to implement the public interest and in the organisational design of that task in line with values of the good administration principle, such as transparency, efficiency and uniformity of action parameters, all of which are aspects of *administrative discretion,* i.e. not permeable or scrutinisable by judicial control.

This model has been supplanted by the *juridicisation and judicialisation of public policies* in the name of guaranteeing their conformity with *fundamental* and *human rights*, all of which carry an *ethos that can be traced back* to safeguarding the *dignity of the human person.* As a result, according to the state of the art, political decision-making has lost its *responsiveness* because it is no longer identifiable with the majority, the will expressed by those elected in free democratic processes, but is now imputed to, *allegedly, technical-scientific standards* (whether economic-financial decisions, dictated by economic sciences and statistics, or scientifically based decisions, dictated by natural sciences in the light of alleged majority studies, or even socially and culturally based decisions, today imposed by an alleged respect for irrational self-determination or distorted historical settlements) proclaimed by supranational, undemocratic, and unscrutinised entities that de-authorise, de-structure and alienate stable, ductile and close-knit political communities. This is a process in which *administrative decision-making* has also lost its *authority* and been diluted into mere "swampy" bureaucracies,[1] sterile and alienating to the administered, or into pacts and contracts, concluded following unreasonable tendering procedures, with high context costs and a significant drain on public financial resources in the name of *dogmas* such as competition or the fictitious construction of public markets.

The future calls for the reintegration of the *public interest* with new dimensions of *responsibility*. It calls for political leaders to democratically endorse *political action programmes* based on clear ideological lines and concrete political choices

[1] To use Sunstein's expression (2021).

from a range of global solutions and proposals, so that the voters of a local political community can rebuild their bond of trust and responsibility with their elected representatives. And administrative law has to be the set of action instruments that, benefiting from authority and coactivity, can implement those political programmes in the period corresponding to the respective electoral cycle, with a qualified, well-organised administration and without useless bureaucracy. For this to happen, control must be agile and contemporaneous with the action, which means that it cannot be a counter-power that challenges the democratically voted political programme nor a politically functionalised instrument that dulls the effectiveness of the political programme. The time of administrative justice must be the real time of administrative activity and must be limited to controlling the legal conformity of the acts carried out and cannot slip into controlling the political choices underlying those acts. Above all, this means that the control of administrative activity cannot be confused with the control of the constitutional, European and international conformity of the political programme, which—if it is considered useful—must be considered in its own right.

Second Conclusive Triad: "Public Administration—Governance—Executive Government"
Administrative law was born in the context of the generalisation of the powers of a growing state administration, which was powerful, repressive, *manu militari* and intrinsically linked to the implementation of political options determined by state political power. It is in this context of "internal politics" that the binomial constitutional law and administrative law developed mutually—these two branches of law, one associated with the definition of institutional designs adjusted to the guarantee of liberal and democratic values, the other designed to make the former operational within the framework of the choices made by the power to administer and under judicial control to ensure both respect for the law and the fundamental guarantees of the administered.

At the moment, this binomial has lost its meaning with the openings of multilevel and transnational law and the countless links that are interwoven between what remains of the traditional hierarchical normative structure and what is imposed by the partial and dysfunctional framework of sectoral policies, in countless arrangements within the framework of the international legal order through multilateral and bilateral agreements, framework conventions, the law of international institutions, *guidance* and, of course, the traditional principles of natural law and the (not yet obsolete) provisions of national constitutions. If we look at the multiplicity of rules produced in this relatively limited period of time and take a diachronic view of law in general (and even administrative law), we can see that either we cannot be talking about the same reality and the same area of human and social knowledge and regulation or the evolution of the last few decades has transformed *law* and *justice* into a universality unreachable by the traditional legal method. Perhaps this is why normative regulation has been replaced by *governance*, precisely to point out that we have entered a different reality, in which the binary method of legal/illegal, valid/invalid and effective/ineffective is spreading into figures with ductile contours in which illegality can be remedied or degraded or even lose its invalidating effect, precisely because the rules are too complex. This means that we move into a context of a tendency towards anomie with disparate and iniquitous criteria since simple things, because they are less relevant, are subject to control and punishment while complex and multi-localised things, but also more relevant and more damaging to the public interest, often escape the power to sanction and annul.

The future requires a *return to simplification*, with a clear separation between administrative activity and government activity, in which public policies rise to another level of functional decision-making and control, allowing administrative activity to recover its proximity, the clarity of the rules and the reintegration of the values and principles of the democratic rule of law, with respect for the spaces of valuation that are typical of the prevalence of *administrative ethics*.[2]

Third Conclusive Triad: "Rights of the Administered—Fundamental Rights—Status of the Administered"

Administrative law as an autonomous branch of law presupposed that it was not only the study of the administrative organisation and the relationships within that organisation that was at stake, but also the rights of the administered, i.e. the legal relationships that were established between private individuals and the respective administrative organisation. It is the manifestation or externalisation of administrative activity and the possibility of reacting against it that determines the autonomy and *ethos* of this branch of law and the issues it discusses. The importance of defining the characteristics of an administrative decision that can be challenged can only be understood because it will be submitted to a third party external to that legal relationship (a court or an independent judicial power) to analyse the validity of the factual and legal assumptions on which the decision was taken. *Administrative law* is therefore a *right of the administrators* and not an *organisational right of the public administration*. Even organisational issues can only be understood as legal issues if they have an external dimension or effect since, internally, doubts or controversies (which do not seem to have the characteristics of intra-administrative litigation, since the holders of powers do not have a personal interest or an interest that differs from the organisational interest) are resolved through the authority of the hierarchical decision (by the hierarchical superior).

The issue changes with the classification of a part of legal-administrative relations as legal relations of fundamental rights, since all legal relations are assumed to be external, and there are even legal proposals, along the lines of the juridicisation of public policies, that seek to transport an indirect or interposed subjective

[2] Chad Newswander (2018) presents a very interesting study on the meaning and scope of administrative discretion based on US administrative law, in which he identifies a material assumption of this type of decision that can also be transposed to the administrative law of continental European systems. The author focuses his analysis on the specific nature of administrative decision-making and the attributes available to administrative officials in order to explain why certain aspects of this decision cannot be scrutinised by the courts. In our opinion, and in line with our proposal, this is a more correct understanding of what the qualification of the administrative decision should be and why judicial control should not and cannot replace it.

fundamentality, or even a representative or proxy fundamentality, into the sphere of inter-organic relations. The hierarchical structure of the Administration loses interest in the face of the centrality of the criterion of the harmfulness of the act as a qualification for its impugnability.

De lege ferenda, it seems advisable to regulate an *administrative status* or the status of the administered, which effectively and clearly results in the different protection given to subjective rights and the respective differentiation, also in terms of jurisdictional protection procedures, in relation to merely differentiated, public or diffuse interests, as well as the various community duties that this *status* also presupposes, in terms of both legal duties and duties of care, and also normative situations of *pati* obligations, bearing in mind that we are in the context of an unequal legal relationship and that administrative activity presupposes the exercise of public powers and faculties.

Fourth Concluding Triad: "Administrative Responsibility—State Responsibility—Administrative Responsibility and Public-Social Reparatory Benefits"

The administration's liability was initially excluded or limited to damage arising from material operations, given that it was not possible to categorise an act of power as unlawful.

Civil liability for unlawful acts, which is affirmed as a corollary of the guarantees of the administered, is a significant step forward in the implementation of principles of equal treatment and justice within the community in which the exercise of administrative activity takes place, and it is now clear that the community organised in the form of the state has a legal obligation to make reparation for damage caused by unlawful acts in the exercise of administrative activity.

However, this *legal duty to compensate for damages resulting from unlawful acts* should not be confused with the existence of universal public insurance (it should not neutralise the obligation of each citizen to seek products on the market that mitigate the risk of property losses in adverse situations) nor with the universalisation of consequences arising from primary political choices adopted by duly legitimised democratic majorities nor with instruments for penalising the community for insufficient economic resources in public services that prevent their *normal performance* or for errors in the organisation and management of the service that does not amount to situations causing special and abnormal damage.

Above all, this concept (that of state civil liability) and its legal regime must not contribute to disturbing the model of economic solidarity on which many European legal-normative systems are based. It must not turn relationships underlying legal activities which involve normal risks and which are supposed to be based on relationships of trust into personal confrontations. It is therefore essential that in these cases of known and foreseeable risks that affect or could affect human health, states provide for objective compensation schemes that are separate from the liability system and linked to the social security system, i.e. based on solidarity and not on tort.

Fifth Conclusive Triad: "Internal Control—Judicialisation of Control of Administrative Activity—Combination of Forms of Control"
This is the simplest triad to explain, and it basically goes hand in hand with other sub-conclusions that have been identified throughout the text, such as the need to once again simplify legal-administrative relations for control purposes or to limit the scope of "concerted activity" to its natural and classic scope of public-private collaboration.

The current possibility of judicial review of all administrative activity with external effects is an important achievement in terms of civic and democratic life, but to admit that this judicial control can be so intense that it interferes with the scope of democratic choices (even if the last word, in this case, may be constitutional) is to "throw the baby out with the bathwater". It is to regress civically, to diminish democracy and politics, to open up easy paths to populism and to subordinate the assessment of public affairs to undemocratic interpretations of legislative choices. A comprehensive reform of administrative justice (and also constitutional justice, but this is not the place for that reflection) is essential to return politics to its "democratic bed" and ensure the integrity of our liberal democratic model.

References

Newswander C (2018) Administrative ethics and executive decisions. Channeling and containing administrative discretion. Routledge, New York

Sunstein C (2021) Averting catastrophe. Decision theory for COVID-19, climate change, and potential disasters of all kinds. New York University Press, New York